The Autumn of Delirium

Inside the mind of a teenage psychopath

Michael Colasanti

ISBN: 978-0-578-00442-6

Preface

Why did I write this book? More importantly, why do I write in general? To be honest, today was the first time I've actually thought about it.

I write to release frustration, to release pent-up anger and hatred. I write to dive into a world that I wish were mine, to explore an alternate life. I write down the things I wish I could do, and I write down the things I'd like to do but don't have the balls to accomplish or try. I write because I'm pissed off, or because I'm drunk. I write to express sadness or depression when no one else will listen. The pen and paper never ignore me, or turn away. My written words never laugh at what I have to say; they abide my emotions, as I am the master of their world. I think this chapter is the most important because it gives you, and me, a clearer explanation of why I spent the hours scribbling and scratching in my torn-up notebook. It still amazes me that this is the first time I've actually thought about this. Ironic isn't it?

Many years have passed since the start of this project, and I have evolved since the start, yet my main goals and objectives have for the most part stayed the same. I can still remember the night I first began writing this—a night that marked the downward spiral of my mental health, and marked the beginning of many bad memories. In the end, I wouldn't trade anything in the world for those years. In fact, I'd do anything to relive them all over again. I think in writing this book, I was allowed to visit many of those memories and places again. I was allowed to look back and laugh, or look back and cry, at the good times and the bad. I know that's the closest I'll ever get to reliving them, but that's better than nothing. All I know is that I had to constantly hide my writings from my parents. God only knows what they would have said or done to me had they found this. I guess it's ok now: I'm older, living on my own, and it's all in the past.

Many of these chapters were written some time ago and are not in any particular order. What you'll read in this book are my "feelings" and "emotions." To this day, I still believe in everything I've written down in this book. I am still a self-loathing, misanthropic motherfucker, and I still have no faith in religion, or a so-called Heaven. My dreams are my heaven, and my nightmares are my hell. My mind still baffles me, and I still have many mental problems. Writing this book did not cure those problems, only made me more aware of them, and I'm grateful for that.

This may sound somewhat strange, but I feel like I'm writing a suicide note. Getting across to you everything I've felt, how I've appreciated my life experiences, and then giving you the "on a final note" speech. Well, this being the final chapter, I figured I'd switch it up a little bit for you.

I've enjoyed writing this book. It's been stressful, and hellish, and pleasant and I hope one day I can do it again. Until I write to you again, so long.

"I hate the fucking world."—*Eric Harris*

The Beginning.
In the beginning it all starts, and with a start comes an end.
This is where It starts...

The mindless existences both you and I live out in this exact place, in this very same time,

neglect the thoughts of why "we" are here. The corruption of our society intensifies what we feel

as humans...and we learn to love, hate, regret, and forget. People can't see these things.

Emotions cannot be touched or stolen. Even now as I write this, I do not feel alone. I reminisce

on times and places so vivid they feel like an almost exact physical and mental reenactment.

Feelings.... I do not believe they are real. They are implanted in us, as are thoughts of

God, Heaven, Hell...and the concepts of life and death itself. The mind is too complex for its

own good. The very thought that "love" exists baffles me, yet I am not surprised. Only the

human mind is weak enough to invent something as pathetic and empty as "love."

I at times feel boxed in, separated from this world. I have feelings so complex, so insane,

that even I cannot comprehend them, let alone express them. For all the good things in my life, I

still feel empty.

Alcohol, Drugs, and Melting Flesh

I was just released from the hospital several days ago. This past week has been hell for me, and

I'm not sure what the fuck I'm doing anymore. I guess you're probably wondering why I was in

the hospital to begin with. Even if you're not interested, I'm going to tell you anyway.

On a night, a very dark night, a very cold night, I decided to go out. I took several Xanax

bars, and had a few drinks. I was rambunctious even before the sun went down, and on a suicidal

rampage. I had just gotten a D.U.I. a few weeks before, so I didn't care what the fuck happened

to me. I drove around for a few hours with a friend of mine. At around 9:00 p.m. I received a

phone call from a buddy telling me there was a party at Camp Rotary, a desolate area in the middle of nowhere where we would all gather and have bonfires. I can't even begin to tell you how many nights I drank my soul away at that place.

On this particular night, I was more fucked up than usual, and frankly I didn't care about my life. I picked my buddy up. The entire ride to Camp Rotary, I was all over the road—driving in the wrong lane, music turned up so loud my ears were bleeding. I can't believe I didn't get pulled over or killed on the way there. Once we arrived at the party, I stumbled out of the car, and began yelling and screaming at my friends. Nothing could stop me on this night, nothing in this world. I began stripping down, taking all of my clothes off. In seconds I was naked, and dancing wildly around the bonfire in drunken leaps and falls. I hopped back into my SUV, and took off into a cornfield. I, Michael Colasanti, was driving through a cornfield on a Saturday night, drunk, on drugs, wearing nothing but a brown fedora.

When I got back to the bonfire pit, I nearly killed a few people, narrowly missing them with my Explorer. I stumbled out of the car, and fell more than once on my way to the bonfire, where I fell in, face first. I threw out both of my hands to try and stop myself, but it was no use. Both hands landed in the bonfire. Drunk though I was, I knew I was burning, so I rolled out of the fire. Once out, I realized I had melted plastic on both hands. Minutes before I fell into the fire, someone had thrown a plastic recycling bin into the fire. I landed in the bin. One of my friends ran over and started pouring 5 O'Clock vodka over both of my hands to disinfect the wounds. I don't think anything has ever hurt as bad as vodka on those burns. Somebody called 911. An ambulance picked me up, and the EMTs administered two large syringes filled of morphine. I don't remember much of the ride down to the hospital, as I was stoned out of my skull….The last thing I remember was singing the song *Someone Saved My Life Tonight* by Elton John. I kept thinking, *how did I get here?*

Yesterday's Ungratefulness, Tomorrow's Sorrow

I think a lot about the past. I picture my memories in increments. I'll spend a summer and blow through it not thinking. Then, not five months later, I'll lay on myself the guilt trip of not taking advantage of that time and enjoying it.

If only I'd known sooner, but I didn't. I'd relive it all if I could, and fix my mistakes, but I can't. That's life, and that's reality, but…what is reality? Is it something we can touch, or feel?

Time does not exist—it is a device created by the human mind to cover that fact that we are weak, and cannot depend on our own personal interests. Time is used to remind us of our impending doom, and that all things must someday end.

I think back on fond memories sometimes and I wonder, *Is that really back? Could it be forward? What's in between? Have I even experienced it yet?* Maybe this is what déjà vu is, the facts and structures that prove time does not exist, and memories are just the mind's last set of pictures locked deep away, pictures to someday look back and smile upon, of something no one else will ever know.

Love and Hate

I've questioned myself for years about love. The more bad experiences I've encountered and entered into, the more accustomed I've become to my hatred. Hate is a very powerful thing, and can be interpreted in many different ways. Do you sometimes have the hate build up in your body and mind to the point where you feel as if taking another human life is the only way to feel any relief? You know, it's funny. Hate wins any way you slice it. If you love your hate, or you hate your love, it doesn't matter—hate wins. Your mind is filled with nothing but sinister thoughts. Does it feel better to hate or to love? Who's to say that hate is not an enjoyable feeling?

Deep down inside ourselves, we're all afraid of the dark. Deep down inside, we all share the same hatred, we all sin, and we're all going to Hell one way or another. I'm probably writing such morbid things tonight because I hate humanity.

Sometimes a lack of love can manipulate your mind into thinking things about yourself, negative things. *Am I ugly? Am I not funny? Not fun to be around?* With years of rejection and solitude, your mind brings out two people: the person you know as your *self*, and the other person, Mr. Hyde.

Maybe I'm the only sane one here, because I see the world and its surroundings for what they really are. However, it's written that with knowledge comes a price tag. This very moment, I'm paying the price. I wish I didn't see what I see. I wish I didn't think the way I think…I wish I could live my life like everyone else. I want to be a blind sheep.

The human mind is a mysterious thing. Maybe we are *all* paying the same price.

The Unconscious Mind

To this day, scientists have yet to unravel the complexity of the human mind—the way it thinks, reacts, feels, grows. In a world of advanced technology, I believe the mind is very influenced by very basic technology. All minds differ, and all are still a mystery.

For instance, is the red I see the same red you see? Is what one man sees what another man believes? Many questions, and so few answers. It's said the human race is on the top of the food chain. I wholeheartedly agree but for one small quibble.

We are the weakest species on this planet, for the very reason that we let emotions and feelings interfere with and get in the way of living. One could argue that feelings and emotions are just learned as one is raised in this world. I do not know truly whether we learn these traits as we grow, or if they are a natural, genetic substance passed down from parent to child. It's hard to argue which is right when you have murderers in the world.

Does this mean that even through growing up and accepting love as an emotion these murderers ignored it, and proceeded with their primal instincts?

It's apparent that the human race is very primal, and it seems to me the only reason the U.S. is as civil as it is because of the media. Television and the powers that be have tried to breed us to be a "tame society." The higher-ups obviously failed miserably as it seems the world is getting closer to the apocalypse every single day. A steady diet of television for years at a time can seriously shape one's outlook on feelings and emotions. I know this because it has shaped me into a person very different from my family. The lessons learned through technology could ultimately be humanity's greatest downfall.

The World of Illusion

Life in a nutshell is invisible, because there truly is no such thing as life in a nutshell. The knowledge instilled in us all creates and forms us as a race. There's more to it, however.

The way I look at the world is very complex, but can be simplified into one simple comparison. Picture the world as a card in a deck. When you look at the card from the front, the card appears solid. The card looks promising. Then turn the card and look at it from the side. At this point the card is as thin as the air we breathe, just as the world around us exists. Our dreams are the best way to reach true reality.

Take the dream I had last night, which made me realize the true beauty of the unconscious mind. This dream took me far away to a castle on a cliff, and in this castle was…nothing. The castle was empty of human life; inside, only I remained. Silently I began to smile, and a tear rolled down my cheek as I realized I had finally achieved absolute happiness. Solitude was my sin, but that's all I'd ever need.

The castle was built of rubies and emeralds. However, in a world that was empty, these precious jewels meant nothing. I sat in my throne and stared at the setting sun once more laughing in my head, knowing that I was truly there. Not in the bullshit material way of "reality." I was *there*. This dream was real, and I walked down the stone path of the castle laughing out loud at the mindless souls that I now owned.

The Grapes of Wrath Have Yet to be Tasted

At this current moment it is 5:50 a.m. and I have not slept in three days. This sudden insomnia has left me speechless. With around 30 hours of free time on my hands, my mind has traveled to the furthest depths of Hell and back. An educational experience, but something I do not wish to do again.

The sun has just begun to rise. A brand new day, and one step closer to our universal destiny. My black light sheds no color on me, on my *self*, though the paper of this notebook is so brightly illuminated. Hearing Bach's beautiful *Toccata and Fugue in D Minor* is all I could ask for. The song does something for me no amount of money could. Greatness sprouts in my mind, as does evil. The words I've written on this page are moving. I think I'm hallucinating due to lack of sleep. I feel as though I've dreamt long enough. It's time to wake up, and face reality. The castle is awaiting me this evening. I wouldn't want to disappoint Spencer. Goodnight.

Murder in the First Degree

Today I watched the film *Taxi Driver* for the very first time—a very good film. Very practical and close to real life. Travis Bickle is an excellent character. His personality very closely related to my feelings, or maybe it was our shared lack of feelings. This is the story of a simple man who caved in to the pressures of everyday life. Towards the very end of the movie, he makes himself stronger. He accepts the true facts about this fucked up world. He decides that the only true way to clean this world is to rid the world of the scum. "One day a real rain will come and wash all this trash off the streets."

He does exactly that. At the end of the film, he murders three men. He murders three men in cold blood, and the men who were murdered deserved this. These men deserved to die. It was murder in the first degree. Murder in the first degree, and it was sheer genius.

I find it funny how murder, no matter how or why it's committed, is illegal. Yet we live in a society that embraces murder and violence on television. The motherfuckers on Capitol Hill then throw the excuse in our faces, "that's fantasy, this is reality." And why do we love it, eat it up, every person who's blown away? Every man who's hacked to death, agree or disagree, you know deep down you love it.

Darker Than Black

It's another night where the world seems to stop turning. Each day drags, and every one feels identical. The petty things I do are merely items to insure my sanity. I would even go as far as saying I question that now, my sanity, that is. It's been a year since suicide was attempted and I visited the mental home.

Suicide has lost its flavor and death is no longer an option. Only the fascinations of life that keep me going: Why are we here? What brought us here? And who, in the very end, controls our fate? I guess you could say it doesn't matter anymore. Ha ha.

Clear Windows, and a Blue Sky

As the clock turns I speak in tongue and no one can understand me.

The cigarette burns all the way down to the butt.

The lights burn dim as the monsters fade away.

The blue fur is screaming, and I want to pull my head away.

Ghosts from the past direct my mind.

My heart is filled with a hatred no one can fuck with.

Another Day in Hell

Every day, every fucking thing seems the same. Maybe I'm wrong in saying the chocolaty taste of suicide has leaked out of my mouth. I'm sitting in school right now, and I can see the simplicity of mankind through my eyes. The ignorance of the human mind. The very stupidity that makes us human. I don't know why, but a wave of anger and hatred has washed over me as of late. I've been thinking about going down in history for something extraordinary. Ideas are yet to be determined, but I've come to the conclusion now that if anyone were to find this book, I would be locked away for a long time. I can't help these feelings. I need to break free from this shit. Bullshit, that's all this is. I don't understand any of it. Pointless, it's all pointless. If I'm going to die someday, I might as well die in chaos and insanity.

Empty Heart, Empty Mind

Over time, some things get better, some things get worse. One downward spiral to Hell is drugs. I'm watching young lives right now fall apart due to drugs and the enjoyment it brings them. I've realized, at this point, that drugs are not for me. I guess it's all a part of adolescence to experiment and discover the joys and sometimes horrors of life.

The War With Reality

The chemical imbalance of the teenage mind, added with the pressures of every day life is a chore in itself. Mix that with the swirling colors of reality, and you've got trouble.

Long nights and a head full of worry are a lot for anyone to deal with. Many have said that these feelings I have are just typical adolescent rage, teenage hatred. "It's all part of growing up." I don't know if I'll ever beat these feelings. They come and they go…but they always return for me in my dreams. Every night I see them, feel them, toying with my mind.

I always think about hitting the lottery or somehow obtaining millions of dollars. I often wonder if it would change me. I wonder if I would still feel the same way. Doesn't really matter I guess. The war with reality is a constant battle in many aspects. Like Gene Wilder said as Willy Wonka, "We are the music makers, and we are the dreamers of the dreams." That statement wholeheartedly defines this entire planet. Everything starts with a dream. Who's to say what reality is, and what dreams are? My dreams are my reality, and my so-called reality, is my nightmare.

Beauty belongs to the beholder, and I as the beholder see beauty as something very different from what most people see.

The war with reality is an endless battle that cannot be won, so I've come to the conclusion that I'm just not going to fight it anymore.

The Autumn of Delirium

The Autumn of Delirium is a term I use to describe one autumn several years ago when my entire life changed. Things were never the same. Every autumn since that one has been filled with feelings of misdirection, emptiness, and most of all…delirium. That autumn my mind was forever altered—by love, by experimenting with drugs and alcohol, and by depression.

When I drank then, I never really thought of it as a big deal. Now I am 17, and my drinking habits have spun wildly out of control. I drink far too often, and when I don't drink, I crave alcohol. I put a smile on my face for everyone, but inside I'm drowning. I feel my life slowly drifting off course. I know the drink is an addiction, and I depend on it. I no longer use drugs, but I feel as if alcohol is controlling me, rather than me controlling my habits. All I can do is wait for the next autumn to come.

Rain of the Century

It's been a while hasn't it? Cupid's arrow may strike my heart, but evil never dies. Truth never fades. Real people don't have real problems—it's the plastic people who have real problems. When you get down to it, and observe it, less is obscured. In this Candyland of melodrama and sarcasm, there is no such thing as real problems.

Do you ever hear that buzzing in your ears late at night, while you're all by yourself? That is the sound of the world letting you know that it's still there, still stationary, still home. Look deeper, for things are not what they seem. We are small, we are weak and we are insignificant. We live like ants, as the gods bask in fame. The world just wants what it can't have. The world wants salvation.

Close your eyes and you'll feel no redemption. Have I made any sense? If so, flip tape over to side B. Thank you for purchasing this recorded message, because we are the world, and "we" are trying to brainwash *you*.

Slightly Less Than Human

People see only what they want to, and people tell themselves what they want to. I have yet to do it, but I would like to sit down with someone and ask them this: "What is your goal, as a person, and as a potential passer of genes in this world?"

Some will stumble upon the question. Others will push it aside and change the subject. What scientists can never figure out is the human mind, and why it behaves the way it does. There's a big difference between a human and a person. Humanity has no responsibilities when it comes to the world, and it owes society no debt. The *person* carries these genes. We're all people, freaks of nature. We just haven't realized it yet, or maybe it's the fact that we have, and we just choose to believe we're not freaks. The only thing I want to achieve in this world is to one day be remembered for something. I want to leave my mark. I want to show that I changed something, because although change is inevitable, I guess I want to direct some piece of it. Change is constant, and it's a very dramatic part of each and every one of our lives. Yet we pay little attention to it.

The world is so caught up in a tug-of-war over politics, religion, money, love, hate. We all seem to forget why we're here. Then when you think out loud with that scared voice, "Why are we here?" your mind stops and you're caught in a paralyzed state. You don't know why you're here. You don't know what your life means to others.

Thinking does the mind good. However, too much can peel back scars and shed light on an empty hole that cannot be filled. I'm guessing this is why most people in the world lock their feelings into religion. They feel secure there, once their lives are devoted to god. Not a bad thing, it's just…we're not 5 years old anymore, and for some people, worn out security blankets start to tear, and things start to fall apart. In the end, I guess this is what makes us all "people." In the big picture, only some will be remembered, most will be forgotten. One day, walk outside. Stare at the night sky, and you'll know what I'm talking about.

Payne I Am

As the dead walk, the living fall. This is the end result of the human race's selfish and foolish actions. I see this picture night after night in my dreams—a man I think is me walking down a dead-end street. All the cities of the earth burning. Satan himself staring into the eyes of my hollow face. In this place of vertigo, life and death have no hold. Walk through the gates, and you will find the land that God forgot. My darkened eyes probe the land of evil. Where is your God now? Where is He? This is where Spencer resides at night. I visit this place as if it were my vacation spot. I am the only one left; I'm the last of my kind. Humans are extinct. The Devil laughs in my face as I walk alone, knowing my eternal fate. It's Hell on earth. Where's my Lord now? These eyes leaving a burning imprint on my mind. Even the moon weeps. I can hear the cries, even from so far away. Will I ever leave here? I hope I do. All I can say now is that I'll be back again tomorrow night in the same nightmare. Goodnight, and welcome…to the land that God forgot.

Moonlight Sonata II

It's not reality that shapes you and me. It's not love that shapes you and me. It's illusion that shapes you and me, and it's our nightmares that shape us all. Everything comes out now, and our cards will be laid down in front of the dealer.

Does your head ever fill with a symphonic noise so sweet and sickening? You know you love it, yet you know it's wrong and you try to shake it out. The moon casts an eerie shadow on the streets at night, but the sun's descent is far more cynical. It's almost like a hand waving goodbye, before the demons have their fun murdering the rest of us.

A Twisted Life

The way the dream started, I don't exactly remember. All I know is this: I was fed up with this life. I decided I wanted to start over, to start a new life. I waited until nighttime, which would give me the best chance of escaping unseen.

I decided to leave on a Friday night. I would start my new life during the weekend. I crept to the back door wall hoping my roommate Mike wouldn't hear me sneaking out. I stripped down to my boxers, and quietly tiptoed out of the back door. Once I was outside of the house, I ran. I ran into the woods as fast as I could. In no time at all I was covered in mud and leaves. I kept looking back to make sure I wasn't being followed. Once I was a mile or so away, I knew I had made it. I ran through backyards and parking lots into a new world. I had escaped a life of constriction and bondage. No more collared shirts and proper attire. No more nine-to-five jobs. I was free.

Later that night, I decided to torment my father. I went to the apartment complex in which he was staying to terrorize him and his wife. I wanted him to know I was free, and that I was beyond capture. When I arrived at the apartment complex, I noticed something very unusual. All of the apartments' residents had their beds out on their balconies. Everyone was sleeping side-by-side, bed-to-bed. All of the beds, so close together, lined up in rows, reminded me of the cover to Pink Floyd's album *A Momentary Lapse of Reason*.

I spotted my father and began my act. Everyone was sleeping on the second floor, so it was toward the second floor that I jumped. I began hopping from bed to bed around the entire complex. The residents woke as I jumped on their beds. The people were so angry: they frantically tried to grab my ankles as I swiftly hopped from one mattress to the next. I got to my dad's bed, and he took a swing at me. He almost caught me, but I managed to escape. I jumped down into the yard, and ran as fast as I could, making another crazed weekend escape. All I could hear was my father screaming at me as I ran off into the distance.

Sunday came, and I realized that I could no longer survive in the wild. I had no food, no shelter, no one to talk to. I was losing all hope of survival. In that instant, I knew I had to return to civilization. No longer could I aimlessly wander around suburban backyards and cul-de-sacs in search of escape.

I went to my mother's house, hoping to talk to my sister, my only hope. I rang the doorbell, and luckily she answered the door. I explained what had happened, and she was sympathetic to my situation. She drove me up to the bank so I could withdraw some money; I was very hungry, having been out in the wild for several days with no food.

We drove from the bank to a strip club down the street from my mother's house—in "reality," this strip club does not exist—and my sister dropped me off at the front door. I headed in. I'm not sure where it came from, but I noticed I was wearing my trench coat, and was armed with my shotgun, and my assault rifle. I walked inside thinking there would be no way in hell the bouncers would let me in due to the fact that I was only 20.

To my surprise, the bouncers let me right in, as if I were some sort of celebrity. I slowly crept into the old strip club. Lights were flashing and flickering; slot machines were ringing and laughing. The strip club was nearly empty, with only a few lost souls sitting in the corners by themselves, but no one living. I walked over to a small room with mirrors on every wall, as well as on the floor and ceiling. I stood still and stared at myself for a moment. In the mirrors I saw a hand come over my shoulder, and a face appear behind me, a face I had not seen in many years.

Teri-Lynn was standing behind me, smiling a devilish grin. She looked wonderful. She kissed my cheek, and an orgasm washed over my body.

Part two: Flowers for the Dead

I was on a small basketball court and wearing rollerblades. There were several other young guys on the court, skating around, playing roller hockey, going back and forth, laughing—everything in slow motion. I noticed that I, too, had a stick, and decided to join them. After several minutes of playing, I recognized one of the other guys on the court as someone I had seen in a movie: Michael Cera, from the film *Superbad*.

Everyone continued to play; however, I noticed something starting to happen. There were too many people on the court. At one point there must have been over 100 people trying to play at the same time. Tragedy was inevitable. I saw Michael Cera take a huge blow to the temple from someone's stick. He hit the ground immediately afterwards. Everyone tried to resuscitate him, but it was no use.

The dream automatically skipped to Michael's funeral. He was in a glass case in a grave filled with water. One by one, everyone walked up to the hole to throw a flower into the water. I walked toward the grave and saw his body enclosed in the glass case. I felt awful. I was filled with sickness and terror, seeing that lifeless body. I threw my flower into the water, and walked away from the funeral, dizzy and confused.

A Different Kind of Species

The human race has tried to pass the theory off that we are one species, that we are one race.

That is untrue, and has no relation to the truth. The world and its accessories are a very esoteric

thing, and it's no wonder. White, Black, Asian, Green, Brown, Purple…. We are all different

species of humans. We're starting to achieve notion that pride is a bad thing, and that pride starts

war. Pride is the face of evil, because pride encourages people to be arrogant. This rejects

difference in the world. However, pride cannot be erased. Without pride, or heritage, or feelings

of pride in one's self, then what's life?

Humans are nothing more than animals with highly developed intellect and intelligence.

Some are smart enough to adapt, and cope. Others are not, and others choose not to. We will be

at war with each other till the day the Earth vanishes. Some things change, but most things stay

the same. We will be remembered as a great empire that ruled the galaxy, but through the course

of time, we will soon be forgotten.

Tears of Blood Come from the Evils Inside

If there's one thing I've learned from mental hospitals, medications, therapists, and doctors, it's

this: there is no cure for the mentally sick. It works much as it does with AIDS patients. You can

prolong the end, and numb the pain, but there is no cure. I try to turn my rage into a cynical

laughter but it makes it worse. Fighting only makes it worse.

Close your eyes, and pretend we're gone. We've reached an absolution so great that the

masses will gather before us, in hopes that we've brought the Messiah. Happiness is what you

choose it to be. I haven't found mine. Will I ever? No one knows. At this very moment, it's

Monday, 2:16 a.m., November 7, 2005. My body feels void of all love. I'm craving something

that I cannot visualize, and it's killing me inside. It's funny—this whole time I've been reading and writing, I've noticed something. I've been writing these pages as if crowds of people were standing in front of me, listening to me, as if I were Winston Churchill. However, it's only me here. The only crowd is the one in my mind, and I'm alone. I'm going to sleep now. I'm going to dream now, where you'll all be "there." I'll see you all "there."

The Reawakening World

A doctor recently said to me "The human mind is mystic, and extremely complicated, yet at the same time predictable." Predictable is the keyword here. "We" study history, but still we as people fail to learn from our own mistakes. God must be proud of His creation. If in the Bible it states that we as human beings are what God would physically resemble if He were to reside here on Earth, then Ha!—His creation is an absolute failure. We're all insane in one way or another. Deep down inside, all people search for the same thing: happiness. Happiness is what "they" search for. No matter what twisted form it comes in—television, music, entertainment—people search for things they think, or hope, will make them happy. We all observe these things to see how we will react. *Will I laugh? Will I cry? Will I smile?* People are given the greatest gift—free will—then told not to use it.

A Cold Day in Hell

Today is far too real to open the shades. It's a cold day in hell, and today I've lost the basis of all structure concerning my life. I keep thinking back to the past, and every fucking memory I have seems as though it's from a past life. A cold day in Hell emits an ambience of desolate, isolated dark noir lifestyle. Nothing else can compensate for its feelings.

They tell you, "Don't be conceited. Don't be boastful." then They say, "Don't be so negative." Where does that leave you to stand? Middle ground—that place of solitude. You're always on high alert, always impulsive, always on edge. The middle ground leads to cold days in Hell, and once reached it you'll have reached a level of delusion that will make this world seem backward. Follow the yellow brick road to get where you're going. Fuck this existence we call the real world.

Intermission

Love is such a very evil thing. Love knows just how to suck the happiness right from your very soul. Love requires time, patience, and caring. Love requires you to open up your cold, darkened heart to everything. The pain is inevitable, and the sorrow and the anger and the searing hot tears will never leave you. It hurts. It stings. It's all the knives of the world plunging into your soul. Our original sin was based on lust, on love. Why, then, is it such a surprise that love is an evil thing? Love is nothing more than undying hatred. You know what God does for you? All God does is take that void out of the pit of your stomach. He makes you think you have a purpose on this Earth, like your life isn't a waste of disgusting time, a time filled with hatred and pain anyway. The truth hurts so very much.

You know, I've been here the whole time speaking out to the world. I've been here the whole time, watching, and listening to the sounds. The cries of change, of despair. I've gone through life after life and witnessed the unforgiving hand that we as people have been dealt. It's a sad spectrum that we look through onto human life. It makes me weary and lightheaded every night. It discourages me to go on. I try to explain to myself that life is the most precious and valuable gift granted and given to me. It's hard to look at it that way when the very fabric of existence is based on our souls being tormented for the enjoyment of a few.

Many of you will read this and think that I am the kind of person who tends to be negative, to always looking at the bad things in life. That is not at all the kind of person I am. I'm always laughing. I have many friends, and I have a very active social life. However, these things are only a substitute for the realities of hardship, anger, hate, and sorrow—the things that make up the real truths. Positive, upbeat people just avoid looking at these areas, and pretend that they do not exist. There is nothing wrong with this. I'm sure it makes the journey down life's path much, much easier. But I, however, cannot ignore these truths. I can camouflage them, and even at times forget them for a short while. True, life is a very delicate and precious thing, but like other things, life in the wrong hands leads to sorrow, and hatred that was never meant to be seen in such abundance. Anyone with some intelligence should clearly be able to see that there has been too much life given to the wrong people in this world. There are too many evil things heard and seen in this world to cast doubt on the existence of the Devil. He watches and observes every move we make, and he intends and loves to capitalize on our mistakes, our successes, and our downfalls. Promise me this will soon end but end in happiness, not sorrow or anger or hate or pain. Dr. Jekyll and Mr. Hyde are inside me.

Death is Not Defeat

You know this feeling all too well. We as a society at one time or another have experienced the feeling of loss. The process of grieving is a painful gauntlet to pass through. Both you and I have felt some type of love, anger, or even hate slip through our fingers as life's biological clock ticks. It's not the people we miss; it's their masks—their faces—we miss. That and the memories we shared with them. We know that these are things we may never recover. If you remove our masks, we are nothing more than a state of matter. It's the physical world that we wish to recreate in a mental state. We all share the same fears. You may not admit it, but deep down, you know this to be true. Love is not a world: it's an artificial feeling that we are taught at a very young age to believe is bliss, to be an absolution. I've always wondered: are our minds are blank chalkboards at birth, or is our fate written there from the day were conceived? It's something we will never find out. The masks, I want to tear them off sometimes. It's always Halloween here. Loss is a form of change, and even good change is scary. Death as well is a form of change, and at this point not one really knows it their death will be a good change or a bad one. No one knows what's beyond death. Death is not defeat, just a new beginning. Human beings often times thing of death as the end. We're always using that term. We'll all gain our true identities back someday; we just have to figure out how, and when.

Innocence and Infancy

Our five senses are the most powerful things about the human mind. These senses can trigger past experiences, and cause us to relive our memories. Smell, touch, sight, sound, taste. For me the two biggest triggers are smell and sound. Have you ever smelled something, and its aroma alone made you lightheaded? Felt that sense of nostalgia wash over your whole body, and for one single second you thought you were there again? For a moment, you're back where you wish you could be. Time does not exist, so who's to say you couldn't live a moment again? Smell, in my, opinion, is the single-most powerful sense we have. Sight doesn't even compare to it. Have you ever held your arms around someone, taking in their whole being? Do you dream much? Do you remember your childhood very much? Think about it, just stop and calm yourself to the point where you can quietly look back to that day when you stood there and knew you were already part of something much more. A five-year old's eyes are filled with nothing but innocence. It's that very innocence that is the exact conclusion for the world. Perhaps they know something we don't. I remember viewing the world from such a different perspective. When you hear and smell certain things, they take you back. You can take yourself back, too: there is no pain in any of this. Just remember…just think about what you used to be. Do you remember what you used to be? You were innocence and, on the same note, you knew nothing. You knew nothing but what you were born with, the truth. But through years of brainwashing and complications, we've all lost our way. Sometimes I can still smell life's infancy and its simplicity. It's so much more enjoyable like that.

Coping with the Everyday, Dealing with the Impossible

We are kept afraid. We always have been, and always will be.

I like to compare people to a plague, or virus. Earth and all of the surrounding planets are the cells. Earth is the host cell because no other planet has yet been occupied by the virus yet. The human race has consumed and destroyed this planet, and soon, just like a virus, will migrate to the next cell, Mars. We will eventually move beyond that to the next cell and consume, destroy, and move on and on, until our virus decimates the whole organism or we are destroyed. We are all-powerful, we are the virus, we are the sick. We are the evil, striving to populate this cell, and spread our fucking disease.

Swimming in the Shallow End of the Gene Pool

It's January 10, 2006, 8:46 a.m. I'm sitting in class watching my teacher rattle off the regular morning bullshit. You know as well as I do that this is the biggest waste of time and tax dollars. I fucking hate this shit (school).

I've been seeing a doctor lately. He's been treating me for bi-polar and anxiety disorder. He's been throwing pills and medications at me. I know deep in my heart that no amount of religion, medication, or whatever you try to feed me, nothing will ever change the way that I look at the world, and the way I look at myself. Those who swim in the shallow end of the gene pool will never understand, nor will they see. Their eyes will forever be covered by this world of illusion.

The term "swimming in the shallow end of the gene pool" means exactly what it says.

I want to leave the conscious mind. I want to join the unconscious. I want to join the feelings I've left behind me, in a void of time. How can They expect us to go on? How can They expect anything? We want the world and everything beyond it.

LOVE DOES NOT COME IN THE FORM OF A PRETTY BOX OF FLOWERS WITH A RIBBON ON TOP!

Love is a forgotten art.

I'm a True American Psycho. Are We All?

I stop and stare at the passing cars and realize, we are in the heart of it all, the nerve center of a metropolis, of a monster. There's more that meets the eye here. This reality is based on a dream right? Someone else's dream. So who's to say my dreams are a fantasy? That's another truth about the world. There is no wrong, and there is no right. There is only opinion.

The only thing humans posses are these faces. Masks we wear. Without them we are unidentifiable, and walk lost and alone.

The human race is extinct. All that's left are people. People are collective memories. That is what triggers our emotions, our sadness, and our happiness. Keyword [Enter]: Smiling face.

Overlooking a setting sun on the Florida beach. [Pause]. "Please wait: Accessing collective mind storage unit. Retrieving File #6,765,403.... Loaded."

Descending Angel

I had a dream last night. A dream I'm still a little unsure of. I'm sure most of the people who read this are from the New Baltimore area.

Where the Hathaway house once stood now stands nothing. In this dream, two newly erected mansions stood in the old house's place. However, these houses weren't new, they looked very old. The houses were huge, creepy, and even had steeples at the highest peak. All I could hear was this loud evil laughing. The wind was blowing, and a voice was urging me to come inside. I did as instructed by my mentor (a cloaked figure with a hood). I went inside the old house. I tried to swallow my fear, because to me, this was real, even on a different level. My brain was interpreting this as real. The cloaked figure took me into the parlor. I went in and an angel appeared in front of the cloaked figure and told me that I was forever damned in that place, that my solitude and isolation would never leave. My memories of the life that once was would follow me into a void that no one escapes.

I soon left the house with the feeling of cold water running down my body. I stood still. "That was his house," I thought. He was in there. I walked down the leaf-covered street into oblivion. He was the descending angel. This descending angel of hell put a smile on my face.

Second ½

I hate, and I hope that hate hates me. A rat in a wheel has nowhere to go but forward. No movement though. Running in place. There is no forward in life. No backward, and no side-to-side. No ups, no downs, no in betweens. Smiles are so much brighter in Technicolor. I view so many lives at night, so many lives in motion. Not moving, just running in place. People are trying, but it's not working. This life we've tried to obtain will not satisfy the Earth's occupants. I do not care if you don't forgive me for being rude. A bomb about to go off, anger on the verge of detonation. We are a generation pushed to the edge, and our children will be lucky if they even grow old enough to perish. I smile at a setting sun in the distance, waiting for the night. Waiting for a new day, or perhaps it's the same day as yesterday, and it's just on Repeat.

Evil Smiles and the Devil's Wine

I feel the oak railing pass under my nervous hands. What fear lies inside; is my death waiting? Curiosity filled the room. My heart beating faster, the screams are dying.

I passed the bridge silently knowing the hounds of hell watched my every step.

You can all burn, I thought, *love is in sight.*

I realize I'm home, and the suffering will now end. I'll walk among these hallways once again.

The fire burning low, I sit and dine.

I reached to sacred heavens—"Fuck you all!"—as I drink the Devil's wine.

Friday The 13ᵗʰ

Today, ladies and gentlemen, is January 13, 2006. Otherwise known as Friday the 13th. You know, I really don't know how this day came to being branded as an unlucky day. This day of course has no connection whatsoever to the horror series.

I wonder what could possibly happen today? I want you to think about something today, and everyday after for the rest of your life. I want you to think about your mortality.

I WANT YOU TO THINK ABOUT HOW YOU COULD VERY EASILY DIE TODAY.

People blow it off, they blow off how easily they could be shot, stabbed, murdered, die in a car accident. No one can escape death. We all share the same destiny—our destiny to die. Live now, don't forget you're alive, or maybe we're just ghosts, already dead, on this day of supposed misfortune. This whole thing is much larger than you or me, remember that. Fuck you, Adam, it's all your fucking fault. I thank the fallen for freeing us, for giving us a choice. God—he's one I cannot forgive.

Something inside of me

When I drive, when I walk, when I stand, when I lay, whenever I do any of these things, I think, and I cannot stop thinking. What do I think about? I think about him, about her, about you, about me. About us. I have something called anxiety disorder. Somewhat common, but it causes me to be a paranoid, delusional, hate-filled person. I don't have the problem, the world has the problem. It's the world against me; my father tells me otherwise, but it's my truth. My feelings should not interfere with my life, some tell me, but it's inevitable.

I condemn myself for my weaknesses, for my fears and for my inability to adapt to this world. I curse myself everyday for these inabilities. I can see inside of you: I know you do, too. We all condemn ourselves. Some of us just deal with in a different ways. I hate smiles, and I hate laughter. I am Dr. Jekyll, and Mr. Hyde. They are inside me. The perfect way to describe a split personality. I am several minds, one person. I am the clown, the joker, the funny guy at a party. I am the calm one, the one who keeps peace in a time of war. I am the monster who dreams fucked-up thoughts, I am the outcast who strays from the crowd. I am the lone gunman in a crowded holiday mall. I am all of these things during every day of the week, all hours of the day. I am you. I am all.

The Day of Reckoning

A cold stone wall, motherfucker, a collaboration of memoirs and anger, satisfaction and mystery. Sorry, let me start over, my attention was directed elsewhere.

We are suppressed by television—by all media and entertainment. We are kept busy with all of life's commodities, so we do not ask questions. We need a day of reckoning. Things need to change and a revolution needs to surface into our everyday lives. My…Revolution, this is what the priest meant when he said I would one day do something great.

Fuck President Bush, fuck his administration, fuck his policies, fuck his family, fuck him. Someone should kill the fucking president, and his friends, so we can lead this country back to success. Fuck censorship. Heaven, hell, purgatory—doesn't matter where we go as long as we do what we feel is right.

The Funhouse

I open my eyes, and I'm in some kind of funhouse. There are all kinds of carnival-type attractions around me. This place is indoors, in some type of emptied warehouse. There are little children everywhere, laughing, smiling, but no adults anywhere to be seen. I would have to say I'm the oldest person there. I'm on the verge of tears for some reason, I think because I don't understand why the children are laughing. This place we are in is bright, but emits a dark, eerie ambience, more than enough to scare a young child out of innocent laughter. I walk around a bit more, eventually I came to a certain part of the funhouse where there was not a soul to be found. I am extremely frightened. The whole scenario feels completely real, indistinguishable from real life, or what we call reality. I stand there for a few moments in confusion, wondering where everyone has gone. A few minutes pass, but they feel like hours. At that point a friend of mine walks up to me, Tony Salvatore, and we talk for a few minutes. The weird thing is that neither one of us asks the other what he is doing in such a place. Tony asks me if I've heard about Elliott. *What about him?* I ask. Tony says that Elliott is moving to Philadelphia. I nod and Tony leaves, and I am once again alone in the funhouse. More time passes, then I investigate the funhouse again. Eventually I come up on Elliott. I asked him if it is true or not, and Elliott confirms that yes, he is moving away. I am completely crushed, but for what reason I don't know: I'm not that close to Elliott. I can't figure out why this is bothering me. Elliott and I think it would be cool if we went into the theater. We walked to a small, dark corner of the funhouse, where there is in fact a theater, and watch a live performance of the online game Rainbow Trip. I am scared, but at the same time I feel a sense of serenity, as if I am now in a sanctuary. Elliott and I walk out of the theater and into the loud and bustling funhouse; it is again filled with the laughter and smiles I saw hours earlier. Elliott walks away and smiles, knowing he will never see me again. I stand there surrounded by the grinning children. It still feels so real. I cannot distinguish real from fake, right from wrong, or sweet from sour. Something strikes me as weird after Elliott walks away: the whole time I was in the funhouse, not one child noticed I was there. They walked right through me as if I were an apparition. I walk back to the dark corners of the funhouse with the children's cynical laughter slowly fading behind me. I walk away with fear in my heart, and uncertainty in my head. I am alone, and the children scare me. The darkness will comfort me just as it did before. Light scorched my eyes, and I awoke in a cold sweat, unsure to this day what that dream meant.

I do wish I could return there. Have you ever had a dream or nightmare that you wished you could return to on another night? Hoped that when you shut your eyes and drifted off to the unknown, you could once again be in that familiar place? Hoped to find truth in what once was? I know I do. I spend half of my life in dreams—my alternate life. In a sense, I have a life there, a name, a reputation, a home.

A Setting Sun

Today is a clear sunny day. It's the month of February, yet the temperature outside isn't so bad. In Michigan at this time, it's usually very cold. Anyway, I was recently given prescriptions for Klonopin (clonazepam) and Lexapro (escitalopram) for my anxiety disorder, paranoia, and depression.

My whole world around me is being altered, and it's somewhat scary. Familiar faces seem distant, and a raging battle still wages in my head. The war with reality… It's very difficult to see past your imagination when your whole life you were raised on fantasy and fiction. Illusions would be a better term to use. Your imagination is a muscle, and you can exercise it— make it stronger, increase its clarity, quickness, and creativity. When you go far and beyond, that's when you exercise it.

I've been studying dreams lately, what causes them and what they mean. I'm interested because people spend so much time in a state of R.E.M. sleep, otherwise known as rapid eye movement, a state associated with our most vivid and fantastic dreams. Pay very close attention to those dreams. They mean something. Your mind is trying to tell you something.

I met a girl at a local restaurant today and had lunch with her. Her face was so smooth, her smile so perfect. It meant something to me, but at the same time it gave me a stabbing pain of hopelessness. I looked around the restaurant. I saw everyone eating their meals, talking to one another, talking on the phone. So many different lives, so many different stories, for what? To justify one's existence here? Is that the whole reason we strive to be the best? To do "something" with our lives? To have cities, and civilations, and empires? Is all this activity meant to justify our existence here? All so pointless, if you ask me. For this life…this life is temporary, but death… death is eternal, and that will be the real challenge, the real meat of the exercise. That will be the true experiment.

My body is in total bliss right now. I'm numb physically, but mentally, I'm screaming. Screaming at the top of my lungs, all inside my head. Kicking and screaming, but I can't get out. I'm trapped inside here, and there's no one to let me out, no one to set me free. We all wish for something more, we all wish for a better tomorrow.

The sun is smiling at me right now, laughing. It knows the day is closing, coming to an end, and I'll retire once again into my tired head, my tired mind. I'm shaking…but I don't know why. I think I'd better go now. The only thing I can't figure out is if I miss my friends or not… Do I? I don't miss them—I miss time. I miss what I used to be.

The World Around You

My mind and subconscious refuse to disconnect. I feel peacefulness surrounded by anger. Everything around me seems to be an illusion brought on by the media, the visions I was raised by. You know this feeling all too well, my friend. Please laugh with me: it eases the pain.

The world tells you to follow your heart. The movies tell you to follow your heart. Hollywood tells you to follow your heart. That means your mind is wrong. When They say follow your heart, they mean follow your gut instincts. I wish it were true. If it were, we'd all be living in some castle in the far-off distance…a beautiful mist surrounding us as we drift away to a quiet lullaby. However, that's not the way it is. The world around me fading, I see light from an unimaginable source. Please follow along. Your illusions are real. Your fantasies are true, and everything that is impossible is real. Don't be suppressed by truth. My eyes are bleeding, yet I remain. This is not insanity, merely happiness.

I just want to sleep now… I just want to go away, to sleep. I want to leave it all with a smile on my face knowing you will remember. Knowing that when bedtime comes, and your dreams begin, I'll be there, far away, in a fog of memory. This is only a taste of the human mind, only a TASTE of what we are all capable. We are the triumphant, we are the invincible. We will never die: you will see.

For some reason, love is striking my heart right now.… It hurts. I wish it would leave. It is about to bring tears of blood and I don't think I can take it. Happiness is only that in which your heart allows inside. Mine has allowed little because I reveal and see the truth. The past is real, remember it, because it's you, and it has formed and created who you are.

A Weekday Workday

It's 12:10 p.m. right now, April 5, 2006, to be exact. I'm in school right now, and I can't control my anger. "Free your hate, SET YOUR ANGER FREE." Hate is what makes the world go around. Without hate, there would be no controversy, no topics of interest. There would be no differences.

Everyone in this classroom wears the same stupid smirk. This nonsense fuels my anger, feeds my hate. A neverending cycle, NEVERENDING. Round-and-round we go. Over the course of this book, some of my views may change, but my happiness level has gone up and gone down until I don't know who I am anymore.

I was sitting at home yesterday evening watching the news. There was something so extremely insincere about the whole thing. Something so corporate it made me want to throw the remote through the television screen. A projection of America: just because it's called news, who says it's not really a movie?

Overtake, or Assimilate
NOTE

I skip around from a few different stories in this chapter, just thought I'd warn you.

I've been thinking about a few things lately that would seem somewhat out of the ordinary. I've been debating if the views and opinions I have on the world and its inhabitants are too harsh and pessimistic. I had been thinking this up until tonight.

Tonight, I went up to a local Taco Bell. I was meeting a friend there, and evidently he was with a few women. While we were all talking, a person I very strongly dislike called one of the girls. When his number appeared on her cell phone, it looked as though she was going to melt from the inside out. She answered the phone, and began flirting like a slut with this asshole. After she got off the phone with him, I immediately began to insult this person who I dislike so much. She asked me why, then proceeded to call me an idiot.

How can you associate with someone who has the lack of judgment and common sense to communicate with people who have such a lack of intelligence and foresight it should make any person want to vomit?

More or less, the answer is that in this world, you either (a) assimilate: that is, realize you are helpless and insignificant to the powers that be, and submit, adapt to, and accept the culture, or (b) overtake: that is, have such a passionate hatred for Them that you cannot stand to even breathe the same air as Them anymore, and believe that the only way to carry on is to fix the squeaky wheel. Fuck adapting to Their culture, you would say.

Yesterday, a man on the radio said; "If you don't like our culture, or policies, or our laws, then there's the door—get out."

Well, *I* don't like our culture, *I* don't like our policies, and *I* don't like our laws. Am I going to leave? HA! Of course not. I'm not that submissive. Hmmmm…. I think I'm going to go with Plan B. The more I look at Them, the angrier I grow. The more I listen to Them, the more hateful I become. The more I feel Them contaminating my life, my country, and my mind, the more I want them gone, out, FINISHED!

I watched VH1 last night very briefly. I normally don't watch TV, but I wasn't at home and had nothing else to do. Anyway, VH1 had a show on called, *The Best Week Ever.* It was meant to insult and mock Hollywood fame, celebrity scandals, and the idiots who follow this shit as much as possible. However, VH1 is in no position whatsoever to mock any of these things since it panders to the same fucking things. Not only that, but VH1 did a terrible job of trying to degrade all of this shit. They couldn't get it right; they fucked up even the smallest of tasks. It just makes you wonder, it's VH-fucking-1, and they can't even get a decent show written that appeals to anyone except the masses of morons and assholes that infest this world. I guess not. Sad isn't it? No time for pity.

A Far-Off Place

If you look at things the right way, you can see right through them. If you look at Them the right way, you can see right through them.

An abomination, an abortion at best. All these words I write don't mean a thing if they mean nothing to you. Claustrophobic and closed in are the ideal words here. We're all afraid of the same things deep down. We're all afraid of the darkness inside ourselves. But wait…my teacher is screaming at me. I'll pick this back up later. It's now 1:45 p.m.

I'm back. Now it's 10:10 p.m. It's quietly raining outside. My windows open, and the sweet spring air has filled my room. All I can hear is the quiet rain, mixed with a lullaby of frogs and crickets. But back to the subject at hand: mistakes. We've all made them. Have your mistakes in the past molded who you are today? I ask this because I have been thinking about the mistakes I've made so far in my life. I'm not exactly sure what to think of them.

Do I accept what has happened as a learning experience and move on? Or do I realize who I truly am, and admit out loud my inner thoughts for the whole world to hear?

The past is behind me, of course, but its scars remain. I cannot tell if these scars have helped me as a person, or completely destroyed me as a human—very hard to tell at this point. The rain is still whispering outside my window. It's kind of nice, a sound I haven't heard for a long time. I'm going to leave now to the port where it's always sunny. I'll watch the clouds go by as the sun fades away, in this far-off place you'll never know.

Truth is Stranger than Fiction

It's true: Truth is stranger than fiction. It's a damn shame, too. Fiction, will always make more sense. Reality is more peculiar because people choose that it be.

Branching off—I watch a lot of movies, and I listen to a lot of music. I'm not sure if you've noticed this, but after a while our entertainment starts to take on a life of its own. You almost start to orbit around the entertainment, as if it has its own pull of gravity. One thing I am grateful for, however, is that I get to grow in the process of writing this book. This helps me to begin to see and understand the complications of this world in a mature and learned manner.

Speaking of growing up, I've learned something in the past two years. *Life is not getting any easier nor is it getting any easier to accept.* From the moment you're brought into this world, it's all uphill. The most disturbing part is I have a pretty financially sound life. I don't have many things to overcome. But how do others put up with this bullshit? How do they do it? I just can't comprehend how it is that while spoonfuls of shit continue to be shoveled into their mouths by society, by the government, by everyone, they still smile. They swallow it, and smile.

Methods of Madness

It's May 10, 2006, 10:50 a.m. I'm sitting in this old garage they call Compass Pointe, and I'm not sure what I'm supposed to feel. The people here look like holograms, just walking figments of my imagination. The older I get, the more abstract things become and the more confusing life grows.

I feel very strange right now. I took a few Klonopins last night and for some reason, I'm still feeling the effects of the medication. I would like to quickly clarify something. I do not take drugs. Except the Klonopin, which I take for anxiety, I take no drugs. Many people seem to think I do take drugs. How very wrong They are.

Everyone has a sanctuary, a chapel where we feel safe letting all our inner thoughts come out into the open. I am constantly in my chapel, my sanctuary. When you enter this place, nothing means anything. The world is a joke. Jobs, politics, prisons—these mean nothing, because we are not these bodies. These bodies are only temporary. Our minds are forever.

I was alone in the factory room once again. I was scared and she was gone, nowhere to be found. She wasn't there and never was. This was all an illusion. I was once again alone in a factory faintly smelling of welding smoke.

When Paranoia and Fear Take Hold

I'm looking around my room right now. I'm looking at all the pictures, all the posters, all the memories—all the good times and bad ones. I glance at my movie collection and see 100 different stories, 100 different fables all with different endings. I am a big movie buff. I love movies, as much if not more than I love music. Over the past few months I've been analyzing certain movies, and comparing them with reality and real-life scenarios. We (people) love movies and music and such because they are a kind of compensation for lives we don't have. We can compare certain moods, settings, and music with the events and emotions surrounding our present, at-the-moment lives, and see how it all measures up.

Quietly playing in my ears is the sounds of an orchestra hell-bent and determined but with a slight hint of uncertainty and fear. When overflowing your mind with material that isn't real, you at a certain point begin to loose sight of reality. That's when paranoia and fear take hold, and your whole world is turned upside down. It is suddenly clear that your mental state is not consistent with the norm. This is something I am trying to deal with. My illusions are all very real. You may not think so, but then again you don't look hard enough. I think I'm going to watch Jack Torrance roam the lonely halls of the Overlook hotel now…. Goodnight yet again. Redrum, redrum, redrum.

The Laws of Sin

My teacher has just finished discussing a matter of law—the use of seatbelts. As she explained we have to wear seatbelts because It's the Law, regardless of what We the citizens might think.

It occurred to me that laws are like sins: people break the certain laws that seem insignificant and trivial, and do the same with God's laws. Of course, any Christian knows that all sins are equally disobedient and evil, because it's not the action that is the sin but knowingly disobeying your superior, whether that be God or the Government. Aren't our country's laws derived from God's laws? Wasn't this country built on Christian faith? We (Americans) pick and choose what's convenient to do, and what's convenient not to do. We're all vigilantes, sinners destined for hell—we just won't admit it. I can admit it. Remember, next time you're told you've broken the law, remember that you're a human, not a robot. Fuck what They say, fuck it.

An Early Morning Fog

I've often been accused of repeating what other great minds have already stated. This is to a certain extent true. I am repeating what some have already stated, yes, but at the same time I am forming new sentences, and repeating certain information for new ears to hear. I am re-stating this information for my generation to understand.

I understand what it's like to be a pissed-off, frustrated person with so many questions and no answers. I understand what it's like to be the odd man out, the guy who everyone steers clear of. I know what it's like to be angry at this fucking nation of God. Don't worry, we will one day have our revolution. One day, we will have our revolution!

Am I still in control?

Long nights, such long nights. The only thing that makes me feel as if I'm still in control is this cigarette. Time stands still at night. Night is the time when you're most alone. I take my walks, feeling the world slip through my fingers. I take a walk every night. I try and pretend I am still in control. I'm not sure if I am.

Tobacco is one of the world's biggest scams, but for some reason, I feel connected when I inhale its poisons, its death.

I love the night: I wish I could remain there forever. It is in this time that I am most at peace, but mentally, I'm a wreck. Thoughts race through my head as I try and justify my mistakes, my exceptional moments, my life…. This cigarette makes everything so much clearer.

The Art of Insanity

I know I've mentioned the film *Taxi Driver* before; however I feel the need to discuss it again. Lately, I've been on somewhat of a *Taxi Driver* binge. The movie gets better and better each time I watch it.

Robert DeNiro's character, Travis Bickle, represents the ideal vision of loneliness. I have never seen such an accurate depiction of this feeling. There is one scene in the movie, I believe it's Chapter 18 on the DVD, entitled "Late for the Sky." Bickle is sitting watching television brandishing a .44 Magnum, slowly tapping it against his temple. This scene is the most important one in the movie: earlier in the film, Bickle talks about how loneliness has followed him everywhere his entire life. During this scene, we see how that has affected him. It's as though you see right through his eyes. You can almost read his thoughts. Bickle is a man on the edge, a man plagued by loneliness in one of the most populated places on earth.

The Escape From the Mental Hospital
Part 1: The Bonfire

The dream began with my father starting a bonfire, as if he still lived with us. I was helping him move the dog kennel from the backyard to the garage. There was another young guy there, a stranger. It was raining heavily, making the ground soft and muddy. My dad backed his truck up onto the lawn, and the next-door neighbor called the police. The cops showed up and told us to remove the truck; I called the neighbor a bitch and went inside, got onto the computer, and then everything started to fade into the next dream.

Part 2: The Abandon Bar

I'm not sure how it started, but I remember pulling up to a small bar with Tony. I went inside, and I remember not recognizing a single person there. After several moments, I realized that no one was running the bar—that all these teens had just broken in, and were using the place to party in. Once I figured this out I wanted to leave. I remember bumping into Marissa K. I went into the parking lot and saw Rob's van, his creepy white van, like something you would use to snatch up little children. I left to go pick up Sherman at the mental hospital and saw Sam pulling into the parking lot in her white car as I was leaving.

I got to the mental hospital with Rob. We went to Sherman's room and snuck him out of the window after making sure the coast was clear. There was a black man walking on the other side of the compound. I gave the signal, and we ran as fast as we could. The three of us hopped the fences in a frenzy, although Rob was having a hard time keeping up. We got to the small suburban road and Tony picked us up. We headed back to the bar. When we got there, we saw that a fight had broken out in the parking lot. Two men were swinging pipes wildly at each other. Blood covered the parking lot, and I couldn't stop laughing.

God's Lonely Man

It's Wednesday, June 14, 2006, 9:04 p.m. I am listening continuously to a song titled "Late for the Sky" by Jackson Browne. I've listened to the song about 15 times in a row, attracted by its depth. It song conveys such truth, such depth of feeling. Music is such a beautiful thing. Music takes human emotion, human nature, and real-life situations and makes them colorful, vibrant, and—most of all—fictional. Music takes this world of garbage, this world of sickness and disease, and creates feelings of euphoria. Music makes me feel like I can be anybody. When I listen to music that coveys such depth, I feel as though I'm taking part in some other life, as though my life is a cinematic film taking place on the big screen, and millions of people in unison are viewing it—together smiling, crying, laughing, and relating to the story as it goes on.

Changing the subject—God's lonely man knows no other roads but the one in his head, because that's all he can relate to. It's not depression, it's something else. I was thinking about this the other day. I'm not sure what's scarier…uncertainty, or knowing what your fate is, what your future will be. I can't figure it out.

I wish to ignore politics, I wish to ignore problems, I wish to ignore everything. Do you know why? Because these things are not me, that's why. It's not that I'm apathetic, it's just that these things are not me. I truly feel I do not belong in this time period, another thing that makes me a misanthropic motherfucker. I can't exactly pinpoint where I belong, but I know it's not here. I would have done much better in another time period. Apathy, empathy, rules, anarchy, good, bad, sweet, sour, right, wrong. It's all the same. All these things are the same when you take the other path, when you choose another life. I won't get into politics because frankly I don't like them. Above all, I hate them. I wish I were free of bondage, lounging in some green pasture, eating apples, staring at the passing blue sky, dreaming of an evil world—a world with governments, wars, and crime. Then I'd laugh, because a world like that would never exist, could never exist. I'd close my eyes…and drift off to another dream…

An Overdose of Emotions

People sometimes accuse me of thinking too deeply into things, and looking at things too hard. I believe the ones who make those kinds of statements are the ones who truly suffer, and will never gain any insight or knowledge about the vast and amazing power of the human mind, spirit, and soul.

Now the truth: I do look very deeply into things. This is part of my nature, something I cannot help. However, I do sometimes overdose on emotions. Overdosing on emotions simply means pushing yourself almost to the point of breaking. Insanity is the limit.

There are two types of people. First, there are those who are viewed as crazy, demented, or insane, but who do not believe it of themselves—they believe they are pure, the only people who are in fact sane. Then there are those who are viewed as crazy, demented, or insane, but who knows that what they are doing is wrong, or somewhat ludicrous. I count myself among the first group—that I am one of the last few who really are sane. I know that not everyone will or should agree with my statements, remarks, or visions, but I feel that they are right. I am a person with intellect and perception, nothing more, nothing less. I try and separate myself from the hordes and masses of ignorant and infected people that roam this planet. The reason I say "infected" is this: the infected person has the possibility to pass its obtuse, sickening simple views of the world on to other people, further infecting more and more people every day, creating a race of diseased and mentally ill organisms.

The day is coming to a close, and it's time for me to retire to my music. Now that I think about it, it's been quite sometime since I've visited Spencer. Visted...who? I should reveal who Spencer is. I mention him quite often throughout this book. Spencer is not a person. Spencer is my subconscious—my dreams, my nightmares. Spencer is the one I meet in my dreams. Spencer is just a name. It's weird, but over the past few years, I've almost gotten to know him, and of course he is me. Spencer is just a label for what awaits me at night, almost like a ghost. I would say Spencer knows me better than I know myself. Because he is me.

A View of a Burning World

Sweating. I'm sweating. I feel drops roll down my face as I continue on in my journey. I open my eyes. The brown mountains of sand that surround me watch my every step as I walk through Hell's valley. I'm holding a pistol in each hand, and I feel as though I've been carrying them my whole life. My hands are covered in blood—blood of all kinds. Blood of the innocent and the wicked. Blood of the unsuspecting and blood of the wise. It's the final day to see the sun. I walk slowly, for there is no need to run. I march toward my home, my thoughts clear now, and I am alone. The desert welcomes my presence, and I nod in thankfulness. As I raise my head, I can see my home, far off in the distance. The castle shines so brightly. In such a bright place, the darkness of it smiles in the distance, waving its hand, guiding me in. Green mist swirls in the highest towers, and I remember all the times of peacefulness and misery. I remember now why I was returning to my destiny, to my fate. I could never leave this place, and my eternity is the castle, is the misery that lay inside of it. A set of eyes far off in the sunset glare at me as I get closer to my final moments. I have returned, but there is no one to greet me at the castle's gates. There is no one here. Solitude is my only friend, and I will watch the world burn by myself, as I have so many nights before. I climb the spiral staircase to the highest tower. Passing the stained glass windows, where the angels and demons fight, I breathe heavily. I'm tired, I'm so tired. I reach the carpet that stretches on for miles. Down the longest corridor, through hours of anguish, and a lifetime of anger, I walk down the hallway to my throne. The cold stone of the castle keeps me warm. With my throne in sight, I relinquish my pistols to the castle's custody. I sit and look out upon a new world, waiting for the fires to start. I'm waiting for a new beginning, and an old existence to end, to burn forever. I can't stop laughing, yet I'm crying as well. The hall echoes with the voices of a thousand men. I sink into the chair with the Devil's smile on my face, knowing I will return again to watch it all burn, as I do every night.

Misguided Feelings

It was very cloudy today. The rain came down in masses of gray. Anyway, to the point: I just left from a friend's apartment. Actually, we're not even really friends, just acquaintances. While I was there, everyone there shed signs of hatred, anger, and pure human behavior. I looked and laughed, I laughed because I used to be one of them. I laughed at them because of the way they show their feelings. You should never feed off of your emotions when engaging with others. People feel that they are being human, being tough or scared or happy when they fuel their feelings. It's all right to a certain extent. Once that border is crossed, however, you can feel it. The emotions linger in the air like stale cigar smoke. The endless babbling and jabber gave me a fucking headache. Their proud showing-off of testosterone and emotion nauseated me. I've learned to listen first, then speak. The human race seems to think that its power is so benign and righteous that it will never falter, never fail. When I see these people, I know why the world is in the shape it is.

Some other things caught my eye, or rather my ears. I overheard several people whispering that I was an anti-social fuck and a miserable bastard. I don't take offense to that. People can have their opinions—that's fine. What bothered me was the word antisocial. I don't really understand that. Since when is one's contentment with being alone considered antisocial? I don't think it is. I enjoy my peace, I enjoy my time alone to reflect on my life. I already know I'm going to live the rest of my life like this, so I'm preparing. I'm 18, so I know the habits and morals I hold now will stick with me for the rest of my life. The world we live in revolves around popularity, congestion, and, above all, one's image. I've learned more in the past year being by myself than I have around people, the reason being that I have a chance to stop and look inside and out. I have a chance to quiet myself and make the hypothesis that maybe there's nothing wrong with me but that there's something wrong with the world I live in. I wonder if that thought has ever passed through the minds of the suicidal—successful and unsuccessful: maybe it's the world that has the problem, not the person.

A Suburban Summer

Have you ever had times in your life where you weren't sure if you were really alive or not? More and more, I've been having feelings that I'm already dead. Maybe I didn't survive the fire accident last year, or maybe I didn't survive the car accident. Little things have been fueling this suspicion: signs, empty streets, lost friends, and missing pieces to a giant puzzle.

Nothing makes you feel more dead than walking down a suburban street on a summer night. Everything is so quiet, so still, so peaceful. The reason I wonder whether I am alive or not is that a year or so ago I had a few serious accidents, and it occurs to me that I have no way to be sure that I really did survive them. Maybe I died from one of those dumb, drunken mistakes. Maybe this is purgatory. Wouldn't that be ironic? Ha.

Life's doors have come to close,

I hold a fate I have not chosen,

Truth follows my every step.

The Right To Judge

I realize that much of this book seems more like a memoir or a series of journal entries than chapters of a novel. However, that is how I expect to get my point across to the reader. I want to pull the wool away from your eyes and allow you to view life's complex bullshit through the eyes of an 18-year-old middle-class male who's searching to find his destined path. Not through the eyes of his God. Not through the eyes of his elected officials or government leaders. Not through the eyes of his parents. Through the stained glass window of his mental projections, dreams, hopes, and neverending quest for the unknown. We are all granted the right to judge, all of us.

This Isn't My Real Life

It's finally hit me. The other day, many things finally hit me. My entire life has been formed, shaped, and molded in the vision of what I've seen and heard on television, in movies, in music, and in videogames. The violence around me has consumed me and had a large hand in every decision and action I've ever made.

Mannerisms, gestures, body language, clothing, even accentuations of my language have been influenced by the violent surreal world of entertainment. Since the age of 4, I have been playing violent, disturbing videogames and watching distorted movies. I, Michael Colasanti, have been brainwashed.

You, [YOUR NAME HERE] have been brainwashed. Many people will argue that all this violent entertainment has no lasting effects on today's population whatsoever. These people are sadly mistaken. I know this to be true, because it has greatly affected me. Those people are in denial, like alcoholics or habitual drug users.

True, everything that has been written in this book is from my mind, but all of it has been in some way been influenced by some other reality, by another dimension. Day in and day out I have violent, disturbing thoughts pass through my mind. These thoughts, however, are not my creations: they have been planted there. The thoughts have been imprinted, EMBEDDED FOREVER.... I may physically be here, but mentally, I'm billions of lightyears away from everyone and everything.

The Moment of Truth

It's said that the clearest time in a man's life is right after he has an orgasm. At that point, all his feelings become true, no longer shrouded by lust or desire. You know that moment; if you're a man you probably feel it every day.

When I cum to my moment of clarity, I am apathetic toward the world. Emotion does not circulate through my veins. It's as though the liquid spewing from my penis is emotion and feelings in physical form, and these things are no longer in me. I am, right now, in that moment of clarity. How else could I write this chapter?

Next time you cum to this moment of clarity, analyze it, and really look at the moment. The more you examine, the more you will find out about yourself and how you view the world without the powdered sugar sprinkled everywhere.

Rage Enhancers

A rage enhancer is anything that fuels your hatred and your madness. Call this a rant if you will. Call it whatever the fuck you want. I don't give a fuck. I happened to flip on the T.V. several nights ago, and what I saw made my stomach churn. On channels 2, 4, 7, and others were these reality shows. All I can really say is how fucking sick they made me. The whole thing was such BULLSHIT. The laughs, the smiles, and the cheers. The most disgusting thing about this? THESE SHOWS GET HIGHER RATINGS THAN ANY OTHER TELEVISION SHOWS! To know that the American people care that deeply about shallow bullshit made me sick. I almost had to run to the bathroom. Has this whole fucking world gone insane? It's junk food for the mind. I'm going to sound like Ted Kaczynski here but television needs to be eliminated. To know how dumb, uneducated, and idiotic people are…. Ha ha.

A Word From Our Sponsors

I think Paul Schrader said it best when he said, "all human pain is unique. Just because you're depressed, or angry, don't think that no one else feels the way that you do right now."

Paul Schrader is a screenwriter and has done several very good films, including *Taxi Driver* and *Raging Bull*. When I heard his statement for the first time, it clicked. Everything became clear. It made perfect sense. Think about it. Sure, we all inherit different traits and our cultures may be diverse, but we are all still part of the same godforsaken species. I know for a fact that someone reading these words right at this very moment feels the exact same way I feel. I know it.

When I think about this, I'm not sure whether to be angry or happy. A part of me is happy to know I'm not alone in my feelings. However, another part of me screams in pain because it proves something. It proves to me that we have no souls, and that we are not unique individuals.

I must go. The light from the street lamp above is hurting my eyes.

"Rules, laws, and straight lines only mean as much as the person looking at them."

A Fast Food Murder Culture

I recently watched a special on the Discovery channel called *Most Evil*. This show went in-depth inside the mind of a psychopath, including comparing CAT scans of brain activity in a "normal" person with scans of brain activity in a psychopathic person. The show revealed in detail how easy it is for the average everyday Joe to become psychopathic.

One of the most significant, shocking things I heard on the show: it's expected or predicted that 1 in every 100 people is or will become psychopathic. One in every 100. That's astonishing. Think about that for a minute. Say you've got 1,000 students at your high school: that could mean ten psychopaths, ten people ready to snap at the drop of a hat. Think back to high school. Do you remember ten people like this? I know I sure as hell do. I was one of them.

In relation to "normal" society, the percentage of psychopaths is mind blowing. Another interesting fact came later in the show. Studies show that psychopaths are actually wired differently than normal people, almost alien-like to a certain extent.

Don't judge psychopaths too harshly when you see them on the news; that could be YOU one day.

Beyond Comprehension

Artificial moments…all these artificial moments designed to make you cry, make you laugh, and make you remember. The artificial moments I speak of are movies and other forms of entertainment—more simply put, the life most people never have. I'm not even talking about the money. Fuck the money. I'm talking about something that can barely be described. I'm talking about the human mind, body, and soul in full swing.

Does it ever seem like movies are made for the sole purpose of making you feel like shit? Made for you, and the rest of God's Lonely Men to make you all realize how truly alone you are? How out of touch with society you truly are? Does it ever seem that way?

When I see certain movies, I start to remember who I am. I start to remember how disconnected with society I really am. Thinking about these things is sometimes Beyond Comprehension. I start to lose focus and sight of what's real and what's not. The truth is, many things have made me feel this way for a long time, and it will never change, ever, regardless of any willingness on my part to change. What's done is done.

Childhood Memories

When we are children, our minds are like sponges. They absorb everything, with no filtering out of what's "good" or "bad"—no MPAA rating system, no warnings, no parental guidance suggested. Does that mean that viewing violent entertainment at an early age is automatically harmful? Yes and no. A common position today says that entertainment and media have no hold whatsoever on people who commit acts of violence. I scream to argue. True, these images don't affect everyone, but there is a small percentage of the population out there that it does affect. It's like fucking without a condom. Many people have sex with partners without protection and manage to suffer with no apparent ill effects. Others are not so lucky. Some get themselves (or their partners) pregnant, or contract chronic or life-threatening STDs. The same goes with viewing violent entertainment at an early age. Many people can view endless scenes of mayhem and carnage and seem to come out unharmed. Others are not so lucky. Maybe that's the 1 in 100? In any case, eventually you will find one or two whose lives have turned out distorted, destroyed, and Eric Harris-like. The $64,000 question: is this cause or coincidence?

After you view these images for a while, even if you are disgusted at first, you might begin to like what you see on the screen. Murder becomes appealing. Just as children imitate their favorite wrestler, or play cops and robbers, they will and DO imitate murder. No one seems to fucking understand this. I'm not saying the violence is wrong. I would just like people to acknowledge this fact. It's no different than brainwashing.

The person = the wood
Violent entertainment = Gasoline
The world = the Match

Vessel of The Dead

And so the night began. I was on a cruise ship, and a very creepy one at that. The boat was filled with men and women dressed in their finest. Cocktail waitresses often passed me. No one seemed aware that I was on the ship.

Then a demonic creature resembling Charles Lee Ray AKA Chucky began to chase me around the ship with a large, sharp butchers knife. He murdered six people in his pursuit to catch me. When I bumped into the ship's security service, they blamed *me* for the murders. I was then summoned to the highest part of the vessel to see the emperor—he wore a crown, and lay in a hot tub filled with acid, slowly caressing a decomposing corpse of a woman. He told me I would be sentenced to death immediately.

I ran from the emperor. Everyone on the boat was chasing me. I jumped overboard. When I opened my eyes in the salty blue water, I was frightened. A world of monsters lay in front of me in the great below.

Empty Voices

We all bitch and we all complain. When the dust clears, it still seems like no one is listening. There seems to be no way to reach one's desired goal anymore. This is no democracy. This is no republic. This country has become just as fascist and controlling as every other popular regime. We just paint pretty colors over its bullshit, so it doesn't look so ugly on the outside. I read the newspapers and go to the websites and see T.V. The stories unfold on the screen in front of me as I sit there helpless to the bullshit I see. These cocksuckers parade around and do as they please—300 people think it's a good idea, yet 300,000,000 think it's a bad idea. Which side wins? THATTTSSSS RIGHTTTT!!!! YOU GUESSED IT! THE 300! And why shouldn't they? They are obviously far more important, rich, and superior in every single way. How do I infiltrate the system? How do I persuade everyone to do as I say? Or at least attempt to do so with a voice that can be heard for miles? I'll just do what Hitler did!

Motherfucker

It's hard to look in the mirror some nights. Dealing with the truth is hard. Dealing with the fact that I have a drinking problem is difficult. I know what lies ahead of me. I will deal with alcoholism and depression for the rest of my life. Drug abuse, gambling, murder—those just aren't my vices. They've never had a hold on me. Drinking, however, has its claws rooted deep in my brain. This is how it works: I become depressed, so I drink. Drinking makes me depressed. It's a wonderful cycle. I go from Myspace to Myspace page, AIM profile to AIM profile. Do you know what I find? I find that most people are satisfied with the way thing are going. Most people are happy. I could have more money than Bill Gates, but it wouldn't change a thing. Money, as I've said many times before, does not fix a fucking thing.

The first thing I do every time I feel bad is ask myself this: "Where did I go wrong? What did I do to make myself do this?"

I honestly feel that I will never find true happiness. There will always be something there, something hidden in the bushes to dilute and destroy that happiness. An unseen force will destroy my life. Am I being too hard on myself? You know what the answer to that question is? It doesn't matter.

The New House

This morning, my blood is chilled. My movement is slow. My happiness is down and my paranoia is up. I had a very disturbing dream last night. This dream was in no way violent, brutal, or gory. The disturbing factors came from somewhere else.

I was standing in front of our brand new house. My mother, sister, and I had decided to find a new location to settle down. I was the first one to get there, and I was carrying a few things inside. My mother had said that she would be moving her things in sometime later on in the day. I went inside and picked out my room, a nice size room with a window, and settled in. It was a very cloudy, overcast day. I remember my new room being very dark, and the clouds were constantly changing the lighting in the room. I decided to check out the closet and put a few of my things away. When I opened the closet, I saw a few boxes on the floor pushed back in the corner. I pulled the boxes toward me and got comfortable. After a few minutes of poking around inside them, it was clear that the boxes were filled with diary entries, plans, and memoirs. I immediately froze. I knew who had written these things. For several minutes I couldn't even speak. It felt like someone had dropped ice cubes into my blood stream.

When I gained some composure, I said softly, out loud, "Eric Harris." I was reading Eric Harris's journal, and this…this had been his room. This realization was beyond comprehension. I couldn't figure out what the hell was going on. I couldn't tell if I was dreaming or awake. I stood up, and stared around the room, chills going up and down my spine that I could not control.

After several moments, I calmed myself enough to breathe properly. Until then I'd felt like I was going to have a damn panic attack. I thought to myself—again—*this is Eric Harris's room…what the hell is going on?* Images of the Columbine School shooting began bombarding my mind, pictures and sounds I could not shake off. I was in a nerve center of anger. All the nights of pain and frustration and hatred these four walls had seen and heard. Every day of planning, and every day of writing—this room had absorbed everything. I wasn't sure if I felt comfortable enough to stay there. All the while I had this very uneasy feeling about the whole thing. Like I said before, I was not sure if I was awake, or if I was dreaming.

I had that dream last night. I've since woken up, taken a shower, and arrived at work. I'm scarred; it feels like I'm still dreaming. The line between fantasy and reality has disappeared on this day. It's so cloudy today…

Something Further

We all dream of a different life. We all dream of a different existence, an alternate reality. I spent a lot of time thinking about this over the weekend. I have no doubt in my mind about this.

A life without war, without poverty, without crime or pain. I believe a life like this is beyond our comprehension to even envision. Just as dwelling on the existence of an afterlife is overwhelming enough. Everything that is around us, even as I write this, is already thought out. All envisioned for us. We are not thinking outside the box, it's been thought outside for us. We are doing this with the help of others. For you or me to envision something outside of this life is simply impossible. Beautiful it seems, yes, I know. In a far-off fantasy, it seems perfect—whatever *your* version of perfect is, of course.

Frankly, I could never imagine myself living in an existence outside of this one. For as many times as I say it, I just can't picture it. How I would love to leave this life and remain forever in my dreams, and even my nightmares! However, I know that won't ever happen…or do I? Wouldn't it be glorious? Forever in a world of constant change? A place where the word redundant would not exist, and unexpected change is god?

Untitled

I fucking despise myself. I loathe myself. I hate the way I look, I hate the way I think, I fucking hate what I am. I HATE WHAT I'VE BECOME. Inside of me, there is love, but it's covering up something else. Waiting underneath that love, hiding in the darkness, is hatred. Hatred of all kinds. Self-hatred, indiscriminate hatred towards humanity, and everything in between.

The Autumn Has Returned

The autumn has once again returned to this small quiet town. That familiar smell, those familiar colors. Everything is just as it was before. Each autumn is different than the one before it. Each comes with a new sense of nostalgia. The fall children once again awake to a world of beauty.

Behind my house is a cornfield. Late in the day, just as dusk is approaching, everything stops. The world stops turning. Nothing could be more perfect. My theory on why I love fall so much is this: fall brings about the end of the year, a closing. It represents the death of summer and the end of another chapter of life. Autumn signifies something all people experience one day, death. Watching the leaves wilt and turn such beautiful colors before their last breath…smelling the bonfire smoke and watching the scarecrows scream one last time. Everything is worthwhile. I can't even begin to convey the extent of my emotion right now. It's overwhelming. Sometimes, if you're quiet enough in the dead of night, you can hear the trees whispering to each other. You can hear the scarecrows laughing, and the wind snickering in long-tangled breaths: *I'm Back...*

Mary

The sun is shining on this beautiful day, yet I'm speechless, empty, and lost in a world of turmoil, and emptiness. I'm so lost, I'm not sure if I'll be able to find my way back.

Right now I'm withdrawing from Paxil, which is an anti-depressant. The worst part of the withdrawal is not the days, but the nights. My dreams have become so much more vivid, it's scary. It's almost as if I'm living two completely separate and bizarre lives. Here's the dream I had just several hours ago: I was at my computer, and I decided to send an ex-girlfriend of mine an email. I haven't seen her in many years, and I've been thinking about her lately. Her name is Mary, and she is beautiful. Out of all the relationships I've had, I regret the destruction of ours the most. Anyway, I sent her an email, telling her how much I have missed her, and that I'd love to see her again. She responded with somewhat of a nasty email back saying she had no interest in seeing me, and that we would never get back together.

The email nearly brought me to tears. I was hurt by the letter, and decided to send one back in retaliation, to tell her how she had hurt me. I wrote Mary some very deep things, and told her some of my most private emotions and feelings that were swirling around in my head. Something must have touched her heart. Mary agreed to see me.

We met at my friend Justin's house. It was just like the old days, and my heart was shining. I felt I was once again in that blissful place we humans call "Love." Mary and I lay in the grass talking for what felt like hours; I was touching her ever so slightly, pushing the hair out of her eyes, and we stared at the night sky.

Eventually, we left, and got into Mary's car. Where we were headed, I don't know. All I know was that I didn't care. Nothing could touch me, I was on Cloud 9. (That's the problem with dreams like this: You wake up and not only do you realize that everything you just dreamed was not real, but you're depressed at the same time, you're in an awful slump you can't get out of...)

Mary and I drove down a freeway with the wind blowing in our hair. She wasn't speeding, but a police car emerged behind us, lights flashing. Mary stopped the car, although we were unsure as to why we were being pulled over. The cop walked up to the car and looked at both of us. Now, remember, Mary is a beautiful girl. Immediately the cop began rubbing Mary. I was on the verge of jumping out of the car to kill him. Hate and anger filled my heart. This fat, bald cop was about to steal all my happiness, take all hope out of my heart, and crush my soul.

Seconds later, a car passed by that was absolutely flying. The cop ran back to his car to catch the speeding car that had ripped past us, and Mary and I began laughing at our luck. This was an evening out of a storybook, and we couldn't have been happier.

Mary and I arrived at a party, where I found I didn't know one person, held outside some sort of dirt castle. I went inside and immediately everyone began staring at Mary, as if they wanted to fuck her. I began to grow extremely jealous. Mary sat down with some guy, and my blood began to boil. I walked away and pretended to understand what was going on.

There were two differently colored groups in the party, red and blue. I walked into the bathroom at one point, and one of the guys in blue wanted to fight me—a big guy, probably 6-foot-4. He started shoving me. I must have pissed him off when I told Mary to stop talking to him.

I beat the hell out of this gentleman, and walked away with great self-esteem, and pride. I returned to Mary, ready to leave the party. I kissed her gently, and savored every single second we shared.

Mary and I hopped back into her car and fled, driving down the star-filled road, enjoying the night gaze, as so many young lovers do. I was bound in eternal happiness, and not the almighty Creator himself could have stopped that. I loved Mary with all my soul, and nothing could come in between that. I don't think anything felt quite like it.

The last thing the both of us saw was the dark blue morning sky as we vanished into the distance. Another dream, I forever remember, and forever hold in the darkened vaults of my mind.

Demolition Derby
Part One: Getting Even with the People You Hate

I was cruising around VG's grocery store parking lot in New Baltimore. I can't remember who I was with—maybe Tony, or Mike. I was doing doughnuts, and circling the parking lot violently, when all of a sudden, I saw a familiar face. This was no ordinary face—this was a face I wanted to hurt, that of a guy by the name of Justin. He spotted me. Justin was looking at me as if trying to intimidate me, but it had little effect. He was going out of his way to look tough. I could see right through his charade. The both of us pulled out of the VG parking lot, and drove across the street passing the post office. I sped around him, and began slamming into his car with mine. The intimidating look Justin once wore on his face was now gone, replaced by a look of horror glued to his face, and he frantically tried to control his piece-of-shit car. He was screaming at me, pleading with me, begging me to stop. The more he screamed, the more I enjoyed the whole thing. All seemed to disappear.

Part Two: Goodbye Dad

I was sitting outside of a home on some sort of suburban ranch. Tumbleweeds were blowing across my street, and there were longhorn skulls lying in my yard. There was no lawn. The wind was blowing lightly across my skin as sat in a lawn chair in the driveway, wondering where I was. I decided that I must have moved from Michigan and bought a house in Texas.

Everything seemed to be all right until I began to hear loud sirens screaming in the distance. I looked down the street, and saw several police cars speeding toward me. I assumed they were coming after me for what I had done to Justin back in Michigan God knows when, but when the squad cars got closer, I realized that they were chasing someone. The car being chased slid into my front yard; the fugitive got out of the car, and ran toward my house. He ran to the porch, and opened up the front door and dove inside. The police were close behind him, screaming at him to stop. The man grabbed my father, who had been standing close to the front door, and put a gun to his head. The fugitive slammed the door, and showed the police through the side windows that he had a hostage. Meanwhile, I was still sitting in the lawn chair on the driveway wondering what exactly was going on. The fugitive didn't hold my dad hostage for very long…. I had to watch my father die, and there was nothing I could do.

Part Three: Seeing Double

I was back at my home in Michigan, and I was in the woods behind my pole barn. I don't know why, but I was trying to dig a hole. I could not seem to get the whole dug, and panic was washing over me in slow but constant waves, and a feeling of impending doom filled my soul. As I stood there cursing and swearing, a person I have not seen in a while walked up. Katie was standing there, smiling, asking me what I was doing. I looked at her and smiled back—what I said, I don't remember. After a moment or so, I realized that Katie was not alone; her twin sister was with her. (In "reality" she has no twin.) I asked no questions. The three of us carried on a conversation for quite some time, and I forgot all about digging the whole. My father was in the driveway waxing and washing a fishing boat that was not his. This dream was the most peculiar of the three that I had; I don't understand it at all. Still, it was good to see Katie since it's been so long since I've seen her.

The Pond

The night air was quiet and warm. The sky was clear, and the moon shone brightly. I was walking through the country along a dirt path. My destination? I wasn't sure. I remember craving a cigarette, but I didn't have any, and I could not make them appear in my hand. I'm not very good at lucid dreaming yet.

As I continued down the path, I heard a loud rumbling behind me. I turned around to see a large white pickup truck. The truck had to be a diesel considering all the noise it was making. My eyes widened in confusion. Not because of the truck itself, but because of what was on top of the truck: a 40-foot boat—a boat four times the size of the truck, which looked incredibly ridiculous. The driver stared straight ahead and drove past me disappearing into the night, and I continued on my walk.

Some time later, I came to my final destination in the dream. I was standing in front of a small pond, but it was here that things changed without warning. Here, the air was no longer warm, but chilled by death. The trees were bare, and the wind was blowing hard. There were people in the pond, bathing, and laughing, splashing water back and forth like kids in a pool. I stood there, confused, unsure as to what I should do. I remained still until I heard the truck rumbling behind me again. I turned around to see the pickup truck with the boat once again coming up behind me. He passed slowly, but suddenly hit the gas and lost control of the truck, slamming into a telephone pole directly next to the pond. The whole thing happened so fast, I didn't have time to react. The telephone pole swayed back and forth for a minute before finally falling directly into the pond. I could see it happening in slow motion; watching the electrified pole fall into the water was like seeing a car accident happen in the middle of winter time. You can see the cars sliding into each other, but there's nothing in the world you can do. The people in the pond didn't even seem to notice the falling telephone pole. They were still laughing and giggling, though I knew they would not for long.

The pole hit the water with a giant splash, and immediately everyone began screaming, and crying. Everyone inside the pond began to burn and shake. Women and children screaming, almost loud enough to make my ears hurt. All I could do was stand there and watch them die, watch them fry. If I were to jump in, I myself would be electrocuted. I stood on the shore watching everyone slowly cook. After a minute or two, silence reigned supreme. I heard nothing. All I could smell was burnt hair, and the flesh of a burned human being. I stared into the sky, and noticed that the full moon was still shining, smiling at me.

The Darkened Movie Theater

My consciousness came into play, and I was standing in line for a *Star Wars* movie—I can't recall which one. I purchased one ticket for the late showing and a large popcorn to dine on. I entered the movie theater and quickly noticed I was the only one inside of the large room. The theater itself was of great architecture, with high marble ceilings and beautiful concrete pillars just like an age old cathedral.

I sat down in an empty seat, and noticed the film had already started, but it turned out not to be *Star Wars* after all. I was actually in a dream and *watching* a dream, one of my dreams from several months previous. I couldn't comprehend. I began making hand motions very similar to those Robert DeNiro made in the film *Taxi Driver*, pointing at the screen and making gestures with my fingers.

Nevertheless, I kept eating my salted buttery popcorn as if nothing out of the ordinary were happening. To tell you the truth, I don't think I've ever had popcorn as good as that I had in that theater. It was absolutely perfect. While in the theater, I felt so lonely, as if I were the only person left on this wasted rock. I sat there waiting for other people to come in and view the movie, but no one did. Then it dawned on me…I'm inside my mind, and no one is coming. No one is coming for me, and I'm all alone. I felt so lonely I could die. I won't go as far as to say it was a bad feeling. I won't say I enjoyed it either. Again, this feeling, like so many others, is what I like to call "beyond comprehension." Things I will never understand.

After the movie, I journeyed to a strange house. There was a girl inside. I explained to her about the movie I had just seen. She smiled and asked me if I'd like to go back to the theater to view the movie once again. I agreed, and she smiled again. She was so pretty. I remember exactly what she said to me: "Wouldn't you like to go to the movies with a creamy blonde-haired girl?" I took her hand, and we walked out of the house. That's when I opened my eyes and woke up. The strangest part about dream was that when I woke up I could've sworn I had popcorn kernels stuck in between my teeth….

Lost Between The Worlds

That place…that place in which you cannot tell where fantasy ends and reality begins. The walls in this room aren't real, nor are the rules by which I live. I'm lost between the worlds. My mind is what creates the music, and it's my mind that creates the destruction in which I see, hear, and smell.

Alone in a dark factory smelling faintly of weld smoke. I have been here before. Cold concrete pillars line this industrial palace. This is the world I am stuck in. This is the place I cannot escape. This metal-lined graveyard I speak of is my mind, my head. A hallway of drawers filled with memories, stacked with happiness, haunted by nightmares.

If what I speak of confuses you, raise your hand. It confuses me, too. Running through the darkness…I've been running through the darkness for a long time, and all that I see is the unknown.

That quiet office room…the "Reception Room." Sitting there on the old couch waiting quietly for "her." I will sit there for all eternity. For some reason, I know she will not show, but still I will sit there alone until the end of time, until the dream fades away just as it does every night.

The Gun Show

I was in some type of small department store filled with shelves and shelves of boxes and black plastic cases. A man stood in the center of the store surrounded by a square-shaped counter. I recognized him immediately. He was a man I'd seen in reality several days prior in a pizza shop in Hale, Michigan.

He asked me what type of weapon I'd like, but I didn't quite understand. I looked around, confused, and realized what he was talking about. The stored was stacked with an arsenal of rifles, pistols—you name it, it was there. The man smiled and turned around, allowing me to browse the musty department store for a boom stick capable of destruction *Beyond Comprehension.*

I slowly walked through the store looking at the rows of black plastic cases. I could actually smell the plastic. I walked back to the counter, and saw something that stopped my heart. It was a shotgun, a double-barreled sawed-off shotgun almost identical to the one Dylan Klebold used in the Columbine Massacre. After a closer look I realized it was the same gun. It was sitting on display as if it were some kind of trophy, as the way a person who deer hunts would show off a deer mount. I didn't even dare pick it up. How creepy, how chilling.

The automatic doors at the entrance slid open and my mother and sister emerged. They walked toward the counter where I was standing. My mother asked me what I was doing. I answered her with a light, joyous voice, "I'm looking for the right one, Mom!" She just looked at me with confusion and laughter.

I was dancing in insanity. I love that how no matter how weird a dream gets, you never question it. The store owner told me he'd be closing soon, so I honed in on my selection, a silver

12-gauge pump-action shotgun. I held it with glee, pumping it like a child with a new toy. This is the last thing I remember, as my eyes slowly opened and I slid back into the "real world."

The Basement Meeting

I walked through the electronic doors of the Chesterfield Target. I walked down the aisles not seeing anyone. I walked to the back of the store and had a seat in a chair that was far too small for me. Why I was sitting there, I don't know, but there was something telling me to stay put. Suddenly the overhead store speaker cracked on.

"The WCSX radio contest is about to begin! We're going to play a series of songs over the radio, and if you can guess all ten of them, you win ALL KINDS OF PRIZES!"

I stared at the overhead speaker somewhat confused, but my confusion soon disappeared. I looked to the right of me only to find a small black radio. I got up and turned it on to 94.7 WCSX, Detroit's only classic rock station, and sat back in the chair and silently listened. I didn't recognize the song. I looked straight ahead of me and noticed another thing: a security camera watching me. I gathered somehow that what I was supposed to do is sit and listen to the radio, and when I knew the song, stand in front of the camera and raise my hand. The radio station will then call and ask for the answer. All of this seemed completely bizarre, but I followed the rules.

I was clueless about the first two songs. Around the time the second song finished, a guy around my age walked back to the area where I was sitting and leaned against the wall.

"You playing the WCSX challenge, too?" he asked.

"Yeah," I said.

"Cool." That's all he said, and went back to listening to the radio. When the third song started, my heart skipped a beat. The song was an orgasm to my ears. The song was "Wish You

Were Here" by Pink Floyd. I went nuts. I told the other guy to turn the radio up. While the song played, I sat and listened. I felt like Alex DeLarge in *A Clockwork Orange*, specifically the scene where Alex has just arrived home after raping and beating his fellow men and women. He's sitting in his room with Beethoven's 9th symphony playing on his record player and scenes of violence parading in his head. That was exactly what I was feeling.

I looked at my watch and realized I had to go. My mother had called me sometime before I arrived at the Target and asked me if I could give her a hand with something. I got up and walked out of Target, leaving the lonely guy sitting by himself in the back of the empty store.

I was instantly transported to the waterfront by a long dock. My mother was standing next to me. She asked me if I could help her weld some type of metal decoration to the bottom of the lake, right at the end of the dock. I had no idea what she was talking about, but I followed her into to the water. I noticed something wasn't right. While I was walking into the water, which was about waist high, or higher, I noticed it wasn't lake water but salt water. The water level rapidly rose, and before I knew it I was kicking to stay above the surface. All I could taste was seawater, and it was making me sick. I was also extremely pissed because I realized I had forgotten to take my cell phone out of my pocket. I pulled it out, and water drained from every button and crack. The phone looked ruined, but for some reason it was still on.

I followed my mom to the end of the dock where the water was probably 15 feet deep. She handed me this metal piece of art that resembled a bird of some type and told me to dive down and weld it to the bottom. I did as I was told, and dove. She followed suit, and we soon reached the bottom. The water was very strangely colored as well, and looked almost tropical, a warm greenish blue almost like Caribbean water. I began to weld the piece of metal but suddenly stopped, feeling like something was watching me. I turned around and saw a shark, a huge great white shark, a fucking Megalodon. I was terrified. I dropped the piece of art and swam as fast as I could toward the surface. I surfaced, and my mom came up seconds later and asked what I was doing. I told her about the shark, but she disagreed with me as though it had never happened. I climbed onto the dock and explained to her that I had to go. I was going to be late for my DA meeting (Depressed Alcoholics.) I was supposed to be there at 8:00, and it was already 7:50. I went on my way.

I arrived at the destination for the meeting, but it was not the usual place but at my grandparents' house. I walked into the house, and saw no one. I called out, but no one answered. I heard some commotion downstairs and decided to head down. As I crept down the stairs I had this feeling that I had made a mistake in going there, and that nothing was what it seemed.

I reached the last step, and still saw no one. There was a single swinging light hanging from the ceiling, reminding me of something from an interrogation room or torture chamber out of some 80s horror film. I slowly walked forward and still saw no one. On the table was a box of doughnuts; my grandfather always used to keep candy and different snacks down in the basement. For some reason, I could not resist. I walked over to the box, and grabbed a doughnut. I can't say I remember what they tasted like, but I know I enjoyed it. I looked around and felt this cold breeze, as if death were waiting for me in the basement. Even when I was a kid, that basement had always kind of freaked me out. It has somewhat of a dungeon feel to it. I looked around one last time. Realizing no one was there, I turned around and walked up the stairs to go home.

Another weird thing about this dream: earlier in the dream, while I was at the Target, I had received a phone call from a lady. She had asked me if I was sure I'd be able to make it to the meeting, and insisted that it was extremely important that I be there. Did she really exist?

Why did she want me to come? Where was she…perhaps hiding, watching, waiting…? My dreams always end the same. I'm alone, and it always feels like I'll be alone for all eternity.

Beyond Help

Therapists, counselors, doctors, medications, and shrinks—the lingo of mental health and mental instability. Many people today believe that mental instability can be cured, and can be completely reversed. While there are plenty of doctors and medications out there to make you think you're on the path to recovery, don't get your hopes up. Mental health problems will forever haunt you: even if things change, you will never forget.

I watch people pop Prozac, eat Xanax bars, and rub their crosses made of gold. They think they're doing just fine. These people think that they are ok. So many people use these things like crutches, aids that help them get around but don't do anything to heal the breaks, but it doesn't matter because they fail to see the world in its supposed true state. I look down on these people with such anger. The funny-sad part about this whole pharmaceutical solution is seeing people who don't even need to be on antidepressants or downers swallowing them like there's no tomorrow. I know what you're thinking…. "Who the fuck is he to judge who is deemed worthy of being on these pills?" I don't need to be deemed 'worthy.' I'll make statements and judgments about people regardless of anything. I was born, just like you. I don't need the right. I love hearing people say "Who gave you the right to _____?" Ha, I love that one.

Sometimes it seems like everyone and their neighbor takes some form of medication for mental health or mental disorders. Do more people suffer from depression these days? I think when it comes down to it, far too many people bitch and complain about small, minute problems.

You see people piss and moan about how depressed they are and pop pill after pill. I don't know how people are going to react when the shit *really* hits the fan.

Burning Down The Town

The action stared almost immediately. I was walking through the streets of a small suburban town. Within seconds, I began throwing Molotov cocktails at everyone and everything. I was hitting buildings, people, cars. In an instant, everything was on fire. People were running, screaming, and burning. One man was holding a can of gasoline. When I hit him with a cocktail, he along with everyone around him ignited into a giant fireball. People were running past me totally engulfed in flames. People were waving their jackets to extinguish the fire they were covered in. I remember doing this, feeling good about it, even laughing as I did it. The night sky was alive with a bright orange color. Billowing black smoke filled the air, and I just kept throwing the Molotov cocktails. They just kept appearing in my hand. After I had destroyed half the town, and killed most of its residents, I fled to a friend's house.

Once I arrived at my friend's house, I had a seat. I watched some television, and acted as though none of it had happened. My friends asked me where I had been, and I told them the entire story. Some smiled and gave me high fives. Others looked at me with disgust and horror. Zack S., for example, was cracking a smile the entire time I was explaining the story. The more vicious the story became, the wider his grin grew. I noticed the home I was in was quite trashy. There was garbage on the floor, all the lights emitted a sick yellowy color, and the place smelled like stale cigarettes. I noticed a trash bin overflowing with garbage in the kitchen.

Just then, the door was kicked in and police officers filed in one by one into the house. They wore looks of hell-bent determination and vengeance on their faces. Everyone inside was handcuffed and lined up against the wall. One of the cops explained that they had reason to believe the culprit who set the town on fire was inside the home. I was singled out and taken outside. I sat on a chair in the front lawn as each person was questioned. Everyone was backing up my story of innocence; not one person gave me away. My friends denied that I was the culprit and said that I was in no way capable of doing something like that. Everyone, that is, except for one person: Zack's girlfriend, Cassie, was there, and she gave me up. Cassie gave me up with a smile on her face. She loved every second of it.

A cop came up to me and read me my rights, then she then said to me, "Not having such a good night, huh?"

"Nah, I'm…"

"SHUT THE HELL UP!"

I didn't even have a chance to finish my sentence. The officer barked at me as if she were about to shoot me. She put me in the back of a squad car. I was headed downtown…

I sat inside the police station, scared. I was really fucking scared. I had killed enough people to be put away for several lifetimes, and done enough damage to run my wallet into the ground. I was in an interrogation room all alone. It was the classic scene from a mystery/suspense film: the one dim light hanging from the middle of the room, slowly swinging back and forth. Then my grandfather and father walked into the room, both of them wearing suits. I explained to my dad that I was sorry he had been dragged out of bed so late. He brushed off my apology saying it was not a big deal. Clearly, I knew it was. My grandfather said nothing to me. I was in a bad fucking spot, and I was praying this wasn't real. I sat in the room staring at my dad, and he stared back at me. I felt bad, I felt like shit—not for what I had done to the town, but for what I had done to my father. I know this dream was a reflection of my thoughts before I had fallen asleep, a scenario played out in my mind. When I woke up, I was so happy it was all a dream. All in all, I must say setting the town on fire was a lot of fun. Do try it if you have the time!

The next morning when I arrived at work, this was the headline story on CNN:

> Massive Fire Rips Through 14 Buildings
> Officials: Fire Considered 'Suspicious'
> Veronica Haynes, TheBostonChannel.com News Editor
>
> BOSTON—A massive seven-alarm blaze in downtown Lawrence that burned at least 14 buildings on Monday is being considered suspicious, officials said.
>
> The fire near the intersection of Parker and Market streets started at about 2:30 a.m. Monday and destroyed an entire city block of apartments, garages, and commercial space. One of the buildings destroyed was a home for special needs residents.
>
> "This has escalated to 14 buildings, 26 occupied units, two commercial occupancies. We also have a program here for mentally challenged individuals, and we just lost this building," said Lawrence Fire Chief Peter Takvorian.
>
> Almost 200 residents, many wrapped in blankets [and] wearing just pajamas and slippers, were forced from their homes into the bitter cold early Monday morning. About 40 people were left homeless by the fire.

Accusations and Insults

Today, with only several days of school left, my teacher had some compliments for me as well as some critical remarks:

"Michael, you're too cynical—you're too cynical and too young. You have a cold heart. You're far too young to be this way."

This is what was said to me; however, I defend my feelings of apathy until the end. My teacher told me not all things in the world are bad. The thing is, when you hate *people*, period, the whole subject is rotten. It does not matter if many humans have good attributes or not. I condemn them with all my heart. We are a virus, a virus sent by God to plague and destroy this planet.

I, the megalomaniac, lust for power, in the hopes that I may one day sit at the head of the table, controlling all in sight through fear. I shall spread my wings casting darkness on the land, and on people in all walks of life: the good, the evil, the holy, and the damned. My dreams of an apocalyptic world are resting, sleeping peacefully. My words will not fall on deaf ears. You will tremble at the dawn of a new era, where the intelligent and articulate will rise and the dim and damned will fall. I will challenge gods and devils alike in hopes of the war to end all creation, a cleansing, TO DESTROY ALL ENEMIES!

The World in Watercolors

Even in this world of carelessness and apathy, reality still fails to connect with me. Reality eludes me every day, as it should you. My bedroom is a sanctuary, a lair where all things seem to fade. Yet at times, problems seem to be magnified in my sanctuary. My sanctuary is shrouded in mystery. I feel as though it's my machine for viewing the world's wars and problems. Through my interpretations of films and music, I gain clearer perception of humanity's inhumane behavior, and the world's deep infatuation with reality over fantasy—a tall corporate building over an old haunted mansion, a domed government edifice over a darkened castle. It's these age-old things that have created a world painted in watercolors.

Return To the City of Evil

Worlds apart we are, and years separate the fabric between realism and fantasy. Yet through the distance, through time, through the mountainous caverns and waterfalls of crystal and blood, I can still see the city, its red sky illuminating the cold dark concrete jungle that lay below it. No sound. No movement. No screams. No laughs. For this city does not house the living, nor does it house the dead. The city houses the lost souls of the unconscious mind, that dream state we all have explored on dark nights while sound asleep tucked in our beds. Nothing but thoughts and the darkness stay throughout the night.

The cruise ship slowly drifts away from the city and its darkness, drifting into the London fog once again. Just as it happens time and time again, I leave another dream confused, scared, and completely submerged in misanthropic joy and pure insanity.

Rage

Sometimes I don't think I can control it. It takes a hold of me. My rage presses against my chest from the inside, like a four-year-old trying to push open a door that is being held shut by a bigger kid on the other side. My rage begs me to release it. On occasion, it presses against my chest for so long that it gives up and flies up my throat and out my mouth heading out into oblivion. It soon returns, because it cannot survive in the world on its own. My rage needs a host to nurture it, like a parasite living off of me. My rage sometimes blinds me. I can go for months in an unseeing, unfocused anger and pay no attention at all to events unfolding around me, then suddenly awake from my rage coma not really understanding where I've been or how I got to where I am. It sometimes makes me uneasy knowing I'm only 19 years old with such a head full of fucked-up equipment. I feel like a broken machine that you cannot return to the store because either you've lost the receipt or the warranty is up. I will live this way for the rest of my life— not because I choose to, but because I have to. This is who I am, and I cannot change that.

I've recently been looking at pictures of old friends. The weird thing is, I can't figure out where all these people went. Did they just disappear? What happened? Where did they all go? I can't seem to figure it out. I go into rage comas for so long that I ignore everything around me. I still can't figure out how I came to be here even now. This whole thing feels like one big fucking dream. I don't know whether to smile or frown. The more confused I grow, the angrier and more hostile I become. This isn't a joke anymore and it makes me nervous. No one in their "right mind" would even understand what I'm trying to convey right now, especially good loving parents—ha ha. The craziest thing about this whole ordeal (my life) is the fact that I get up for work everything morning, and no one there thinks I'm anything out of the ordinary. I'm like the Ted Bundy of hate: no one knows about me. I must hide it pretty well. It's amazing how many people we encounter throughout the day who seem normal on the outside and yet on the inside they're out of their fucking minds.

Mad World

Spring has returned. Everything is coming back to me now. With this fifth of Jack in me now, I can feel the ghosts surrounding me as I write. To be honest, I'm in such a delusional drunken stupor that I'm not really thinking about what I am writing.

I can smell the warm summer air teasing my nose with memories of a life I once lived. But no more, no more. My English books always told me not to use "but" at the beginning a sentence. But this is MY work, my writing. What the fuck do they know?

Depression is suddenly rushing back to me. That old feeling of nostalgia washes over me just like before. My feelings are once again coming into perspective, and I now realize how many years have passed since that "Autumn of Delirium" so long ago. Even the start of this book began around three years ago. I don't know who or what I am anymore. At the same time, I don't care. The cool spring air is passing me once again reminding me to get some sleep. It's probably right. Goodnight. Spencer.

Late Nights

There was so much to this dream, so much that I only remember several specific moments.

It started out in a small apartment living room. I was sitting on a couch. Sitting across from me was a cute Asian girl with a friend sleeping next to her. The girl realized we were not in the Metro Detroit area. I told her where I was from and she giggled. With the exception of the sleeping friend, the girl and I were the only ones in the room. Dark…it was so dark in the room. A kitchen light was on one room over, and the light was dimly pouring onto the both of us. We talked for a while, then I fell asleep with a lit cigarette in my mouth.

This next part was quite odd, because it was a dream within a dream.

I was hovering above a small putrid-smelling pond. It was early, dark, and somewhat foggy. All of a sudden I saw a massive creature lurking beneath the water, huge and hulking. When the creature partially emerged, I realized it was a dragon or a demon of some kind. Horns and spikes spiraled from every square inch of its body. The creature sank beneath the water again and I was frozen with fear. This scene was wiped away and I was transported to some type of Aztec temple. My mother's side of the family was there having a barbeque. My Uncle Ray asked me if I'd like a beer. My father and Aunt Janet were floating in a pool in inner tubes. I don't remember anymore...

Under the Influence

Staring at the ceiling at 1:00 a.m. Swirling pictures spin around my head like a carousel going 100 mph...faces and horses going too fast to be safe, too fast to be seen...stoned out of my mind, all my efforts to gain a grasp on reality futile. I drown in a guilty sorrow, unable to accept what I am, or what I've become. The night drags on, and I see no end in sight. Very rarely do I get high, and the words above are the reason why. Last night, nothing matched and everything was mixed, thoughts and emotions alike. I was haunted by faces from my dreams from the nights prior...the trees quietly blowing outside my window...I just wanted the night to end. I just wanted to pass out and to wake up coherent and aware of what was going on. At 19 years old, I've realized pot—or any drugs for that matter—is not for me. Never has been, but I felt experimentation was a necessity of my teen years.

I kept seeing her face. Her face kept flashing in my mind. I could not help it. Several nights ago, I had a dream with her in it. This dream completely threw the day that followed out of whack and threw my mental balance out of alignment. There are some things I will never get over, and there are some things I will never forget. I'm not sure if the alcohol helps or hurts this. Alcohol baffles me. I still haven't figure out if it helps my fucked-up state of emotions, or destructively and violently makes them worse. Alcohol is something I do like, though. I like to drink. However, there is that line—the line between stable and unstable. Once that line is crossed, everything gets worse very, very fast. Things quickly spiral out of control and at that

point, not much can be done to save the person in despair from loudly sobbing at a party full of

confused faces. I've unfortunately drunk myself into this situation more times than I'd like to

admit...

Choking On Death

In the start of the dream it was the middle of the night and I was in front of a brightly lit

apartment complex somewhere north of the city. Snow was falling and it was fairly cold outside.

I deduced it was around Christmas time by the lights were hanging from the buildings. I walked

up to the door to the apartment complex, searching my pockets for keys, and as I was fumbling

for the lock, a young man came to the door to let me in. He was in his mid 20s, dressed in tight

black pants and a black long-sleeved shirt. He grinned as he waited for me to come inside. Just as

I was about to enter the apartment, he slammed the door in my face. Confused, I stood at the

doorway for a few seconds. The door opened again. The man was standing there, still grinning.

"Ha ha—I was just kidding, c'mon," he said, but just as I was about to enter, he once again

slammed the door in my face. Realizing he was fucking with me, I began pounding on the door,

yelling at him to let me in. Finally he opened the door and quickly turned around and began

walking up the stairs away from me. I just stood in the open doorway, dumbfounded, wondering

what the hell was going on.

      I walked up a few flights of stairs, unsure where I was going. When I got to around the

third floor, I came to what I believed was my destination, and my instincts proved right. My dad

was standing outside of the party, looking as though he were on his way out. He called over to

me: "Michael, I'm getting out of here. I'll talk to you tomorrow." As he stared at me, another man walked up and began rattling off a frantic incoherent sentence about my mother and someone inside the party. I could tell immediately that the man had been drinking heavily. My dad just looked at me and said, "Your mom is gonna ream your ass out if you go in there and ask her that." I had no idea what the hell was going on. No one was making any sense at all. I turned around and my dad was walking down the stairs. I was about to walk over and say goodbye to him, but three or four people began a conversation with him and I didn't want to interrupt.

I turned and followed the drunken man inside the party, where I spotted my mom, aunts, uncles, and everyone else loudly and mindlessly milling around. There were tables with food everywhere. Wine glasses and beer bottles lined the room. I walked over to where my mother was sitting and said hello. Sitting next to her were Uncle Ray and Aunt Janet. I walked over to the table with all the food, and grabbed a handful of pretzels. I noticed a cell phone sitting next to the bowl of pretzels. It began to ring so loudly that everyone in the party turned and looked. My uncle asked if I could hand the phone to him, so I grabbed it and headed toward him. When I held out the phone, he knocked my handful of pretzels on the ground and I began frantically picking them up. Everything went fuzzy and the second part of the dream began.

I was on a ship of some sort in the middle of the ocean and somehow ended up falling off into the cold water. I screamed as the ship slowly drifted away from me. A swarm of fish began circling me and started to latch onto me. I was afraid. In the midst of fending off the fish, I heard a voice in my ears commanding me to swim. While moving as fast as I could, I saw in the corner of my eye an odd sight: a different ship was sinking about 50 yards away from me. The ship looked like an aircraft carrier or some type of naval ship. Its bow was in the air, and it was slowly going down. The voice in my head spoke again. "Swim over to it. Go down with it." Without questioning, I swam over to the sinking ship and held on. The voice smoothly whispered, "Go down with the ship. Drown with it. You'll be glad you did." Still without questioning, I held onto the ship as it went down, the increasing suction pulling me faster and faster. Once underneath the water, I could feel the pressure begin to build around my body. The farther down I went, the more intense the pressure became. Soon I couldn't take it anymore, and I let go of the ship and began swimming as fast as I could toward the surface. (In my opinion, drowning in a dream is one of the worst feelings you can experience.) I gasped for breath, taking in as much air as I possibly could. A few minutes went by, and in the distance, I spotted *another* sinking ship. I decided that this time I would do it—I would drown. I swam over to the ship and grabbed on as tightly as I could, ensuring death. The ship and I penetrated the underworld, and prepared for our journey to the great below. The pressure once again began to build around me, but this time I ignored it. I knew I was going to die. The ocean floor appeared and I could see the ship that had sunken several minutes before. Once at the bottom, I could feel how intense the pressure was. It hurt—it hurt bad. Again I let go. Crackling worlds echoed through my head: "Now, let go, let yourself go. Drown, and join the others." I tried opening my mouth to let the seawater into my lungs but I was still holding my breath. I scrambled in pain. Just then, a large piece of steel landed on top of me, killing me instantly. Now dead, I was free. Able to explore the underworld. I no longer had to breathe. It was so weird not having to breathe, yet surviving the dark blue known. I was defying all logical laws. I was dead. I walked along the ocean floor, which was completely lined with steel. My footsteps muted, I spotted a floating platform in the middle of the small city. Aboard the floating platform was Lucia Cifarelli, the lead singer of KMFDM. She had apparently suffered the same fate I had. I spoke with her for a few minutes, but I don't remember what was said. The eerieness of the dark blue unknown began to disappear as I slipped into another twisted dream, fueled by my demented mind.

A Trip to Kmart

Mike and I were walking around Kmart. What we were looking for, I'm not sure. I can't recall how long we walked around for, however, and the walk soon ended.

Mike was standing in the sporting goods aisle looking at the shotguns. He quietly mumbled to himself as he sifted through the selection. At last he found a winner: a cheap poorly assembled 12 gauge shotgun, to say the least. He looked so happy, though, I didn't want to crush him.

The next step was to buy ammunition. Mike and I searched the store high and low, but could not seem to find any shells for the gun.

Part Two: The Amusement Park

I don't remember who I was at the amusement park with. I couldn't see anyone's face. I wasn't at the park for very long—just long enough to know something was wrong.

Part Three: Fucking Old Friends

I was walking through a parking lot with my cousin Chris. Out of the corner of my eye, I spotted a girl I knew, Amanda. I walked up to her, and the biggest smile I've ever seen appeared across her face. She began kissing my cousin, and I remember feeling quite jealous. My cousin disappeared, and Amanda and I were alone in a strange house. I picked her up, walked to a more secluded spot, and started kissing her. At first, she resisted, but soon she was enjoying every lust-filled second. I carried her into an empty bedroom and we started taking each other's clothes off.

After a few minutes, she urged me to leave, insisting that Justin and her father were outside getting high and they were about to come in. I did as she asked. I grabbed a blanket, covered myself, and ran into the basement.

Part Four: Murder in The First

I was sitting in my grandmother's living room. Mike was sitting next to me and across from us sat an FBI agent. The agent was asking Mike about the murder he had committed. I assumed Mike had shot someone with the gun he'd purchased several dreams prior. Mike calmly sat in the love seat drinking Busch Light as the agent questioned him. No handcuffs, no guards, no worries—Mike seemed as happy as could be. At one point, the FBI agent asked me a few questions.

"Do you think your friend did this?"

"Do I think he did it? Yes," I said. Years of abuse and torment will push anyone over the edge. He had to do what he had to do.

Running in Circles

Round and round I go, night after night. Chasing my tail like a dog on coke. Trying to figure out how to beat this life. Trying to figure out how to "win," so to speak. I refuse to be another asshole, and I refuse to be another average Joe, short of everything and living for nothing.

For the past few months, I've been sitting alone contemplating, thinking, and devising plans on how to get where I want to go. Achieving the goals I have set in front of me will be complicated and tricky. In a world where so few make it, it's hard to have optimism, to believe or hope. Of course all those things are needed to attain what you're looking for. This is the United States of America, so in theory I should have no problem reaching the top. However, it seems our country is slowing, going downhill on its way to the end—the end of an empire, the end of an era. Just like the Romans and the Greeks, and all other great empires that have risen and fallen over the centuries.

We're always told, "anything is possible—you can achieve anything." I like the motto, yet it's difficult to actually live life that way, with an open mind and patience. Patience is the key word. I personally do not have any patience. I expect everything to come *now*, because if it doesn't come now, when will it come? Do you have any idea how crushing that would be to pour 15, 20, 25 years of your life into your passion, your love…and achieve nothing? To realize that you have failed? FAILURE… That is the word I am afraid of, and that is what scares me from fully setting forth. I don't know what I would do if I spent my whole life trying to reach the top of my goal and, in the end, fell off of the proverbial mountain before I ever reached my heaven.

Some nights I beat myself up for hours on end trying to figure out how to get where I'm going. I pressure myself into feeling like a nobody to justify my lack of success so far. It always seems like it's impossible for someone like me to achieve greatness. You see the faces of famous musicians and actors, and people of importance. You see them and you see Hollywood, and it feels like another world—another world you have no way of getting to. Even if you had a way to get there, you have no business going there, because you are not one of Them, and you will never be good enough. In a world where fame is so highly valued and money is more important than values, it's hard not to envy those on top. It's hard not to shake your fist at Them, screaming and cursing as loudly as you can, "Why you? Why not me? Why not her?" It's a shame, because some people *are* good enough; they're just not given the necessary means to get there.

The Tower

I awoke in some type of dark storeroom. There was all kinds of construction equipment lying around. I looked around and saw my dad standing with several other people I did not know. He told me to put on my yellow boots and follow him. I peeked out the open door and realized where I was: the San Antonio parking deck my family's construction company was working on. The building was a quarter mile away or so. However, it looked much different than the last time I had seen it. The parking garage looked like some sort of palace. There was even a tower on top resembling the Stratosphere in Las Vegas. The building emanated power, a power I did not understand. My father told me to jump on the John Deere Gator (a small all-terrain vehicle) and ride with him to the jobsite. I was putting on my yellow boots, but my dad did not seem to want to wait any longer. The Gator began rumbling down the dirt path and disappeared. I tried to catch up with him, but he was gone and I could not seem to run fast enough. I now had no idea how to get to the jobsite. I turned around and began to head toward the hotel room.

After I got back to the hotel room, I sat for several minutes and wondered how I'd gotten to San Antonio in the first place. I did not remember a plane ride, or the airport. When my father returned to the hotel room, I just stared at him. I finally asked him how we had gotten to Texas. He couldn't answer me. He wouldn't even acknowledge me. He just turned around and left.

The next scene automatically transferred me to a plane. I was in my seat, and the plane was taking off. My dad, who was sitting next to me, was sleeping. I nudged him and asked where we were going. He whispered "Las Vegas." When we arrived at the Las Vegas airport, my mind flipped. At the end of the terminal, I found the new Fontainebleau Tower we were building. Why it was in the airport, I don't know. At the base of the building was a giant crane on some sort of track. This part is somewhat difficult to describe. The Fontainebleau Tower was 40 or 50 stories tall. When the crane came back down to floor level, I got on and decided to take a ride. After going up and down several times, my dad said he'd be right back. He told me he was going to buy some tickets for the ride, whatever that meant. I had no intention of staying in the airport by myself, so I left. I headed toward our hotel.

Once I got to the hotel, almost immediately I received a phone call from my dad. "Michael, where are you? I have two tickets to ride the crane!" Just as I was about to speak, I realized I was dreaming, and I realized that it did not matter whether I went back to the airport or not. My father was not there, and would not miss me. I hung up the phone and lay on the bed. Staring at the ceiling, I fell asleep and woke back up, hearing my alarm clock. I was once again returned to reality.

A Growing Disease

The year, 2008. The month, January. The day, Monday, and the online fad that has everyone hooked? Myspace. I won't bother explaining what myspace is, because if you haven't heard of it, I doubt you'd be reading this book.

Myspace, created by some college dropout, now owned by a large company, has grown over the past few years into a large corporation making billions of dollars. How does that happen, and where does the transition take place? Of course, it doesn't matter how or when it happened. I'm just leading into a long-winded rant.

Myspace has gotten to the point where when I see it I start to feel ill. The people in this country's need for companionship and constant interaction make me want to puke. Through shows like *American Idol* and websites like myspace, constant interaction and constant companionship seem almost 100% possible. Say ten, even fifteen years ago, the idea of a website like myspace would have failed miserably. The idea would sound not only bizarre and somewhat demented, but most importantly, impossible. WHY IS IT WE FEEL THE NEED TO CREATE MINDLESS TECHNOLOGY? Profit. *That's* the reason myspace exists. Profit. Simple. In the end, everything exists for profit. There is not one thing in this world that does not exist to simply make money. Even religion is in place TO MAKE MONEY! MAKE SURE WHEN THE BASKET GOES AROUND, YOU DROP YOUR FUCKING MONEY IN!

The mindless idiots who use myspace, where are they? Everywhere. They are all around us. I think the people who use it must be either

A. Extremely Lonely

B. Following Trends

C. Pedophiles, perverts, etc.

Those are the groups into which I am certain myspace people fit. Sure there are strays here and there who don't fit into those categories. At the end of this rant, I feel like I've accomplished nothing, and ultimately wasted 15 minutes of my time conveying to you my hatred of yet another piece of mindless wasted technology. In my closing statements I will tell you one thing, and make it clear to you. I at one time had a myspace—for quite a while, too. My reason for getting rid of it? Paranoia, fear, and mainly the realization that it was pointless—an absolute waste of my time. Most of my life is a wasted thing, but myspace was at least one wasted area I had some choice in. Which brings me to my final topic.

Big Brother. In all honesty, I have long been paranoid of anyone and everyone, from the local police to the president of the United States of America, looking at my personal information. I was tired of posting things on myspace, then having second thoughts and quickly deleting them for fear that the police or FBI might read or see what I posted. It's funny: none of us likes the government to know too much about us, yet we openly post our entire life story on the Internet for the whole fucking world to see. This is the government's way of gaining access into our lives, of profiling us. Very clever, if you ask me. Myspace has flash and style to it, and at first glance looks harmless. Smart thinking: to gain your enemies' trust, in this case citizens, you have to deceive and fool them. Deceive them so they will never know what is about to happen.

Phone Calls at 4 a.m.

Last night was very weird. I was sleeping, and around four in the morning, I got a phone call. Take one good guess who it was. Give up? Thought you would. It was Dana. I was shocked. Dana was the last person I expected to be calling me at 4 a.m. What surprised me even more was the person she was with. Dana was with Katie, another one of my ex-girlfriends. Suprisingly, I was happy to hear from her as well. Once we began talking on the phone, the conversation began to get very sexual and I was fucking shocked. Katie was talking about things that were making me sweat.

Dana and Katie conveyed to me how much they missed me. I was still in a state of shock. We talked for about an hour. At the end of the conversation, Dana and Katie expressed how they wanted to come over next weekend. I felt like a million dollars after that phone call.

Tricks and Trapdoors

I'm not sure why I didn't recognize this last night, because I should have. I've once again been duped. Sometimes I don't think I'm quite as smart as I perceive myself to be.

I am referring to the phone call I received last night from Katie and Dana. I've come to realize that once again, they were just messing with me. This is, of course, not the first time this has happened. I've stepped on a rug with no solid floor beneath it. They are once again laughing at me. I thought the phone call was too good to be true. I can be very naive sometimes, and it gets me into serious trouble.

This is not what I need right now. I knew my luck wasn't that good. I'm not sure what's wrong with me. I should be a happy guy, but I'm not. If I were to write down what I'm feeling right now, I think it would really disturb you. My lack of foresight never fails, NEVER. For as intelligent as I believe I am, my judgment more often than not is completely unreliable and misguided.

Cognitive Behavioral Therapy

It's been a while since I've felt like this, the feeling that I'm going to snap. I'm seriously fucked up. All I feel is rage and emptiness. I will not tell my parents about this—they've been through enough shit because of me. They are just now feeling that everything is back to normal, and that their son is headed in the right direction. I need to get help soon, or else I'm going to blow. The rain keeps on coming down, and it's making this all the more agonizing.

Last night, I just started crying, and I could not control it. I'm such a fucking pussy. It's been years since that has happened, me crying like that. I won't admit it out aloud, but I'm a self-loathing motherfucker, which is probably the reason I'm so cynical and apathetic. What a nice day…

An Industrial Hell

Look around you. Do you know where you are? The chains hanging from the damp ceiling. The cold concrete passing your moist fingers. Do you smell the smoke? Do you hear the steel falling? Endless corridors of darkness, only illuminated by the swaying lights above your head. You are alone in an industrial hell. Your breath appears in front of your face, curling into oblivion. Are you scared? Are you afraid? Has the blood run from your face? Don't worry: it's all part of your visit here. You'll be gone soon.

Mist begins to hug your feet as you slowly find your way in the corridors. You can hear faint voices far off in the distance. Is there someone there? Or is it your sick twisted imagination creating scenarios you'd only see in horror films? Here, there is no Freddy Krueger, there is no demon or witch, there's just you. You are alone with nothing but your mind and an ocean of distorted pictures and memories. You will soon awaken and return to another nightmare.

The Dark Room

The artificial lights pouring in through the window in the next room give the illusion of a setting sun. It's so dark in here, I can't really make out what I'm writing, nor can anyone else—which is fine by me. In this room, I'm contemplating what I'm supposed to do. "Do?" you ask. "Do with what?" With everything surrounding my life. The song "Burn" by Nine Inch Nails is resonating through my headphones and just now nothing could possibly sound any more beautiful. I feel incredibly relaxed in the darkness, perhaps because no one can see me. No one can read this. I feel as though I've taken several Vicodins. Hmmm…

Shadows slowly pass in front of my eyes, and everything seems to be in slow motion. My imaginary feelings of mass violence and suffering still plague my mind and they have overthrown my life. Maybe if I just pretend I'm not in control everything will be much easier.

Zombie. I am the zombie. I am the walking dead—ha ha—at least, it feels that way. Invisible to all. I cannot die. Have I ever told you I'm a messianic motherfucker? I'm sure I have

☺

Gray Skies

It's been raining for three days now, and hasn't showed any signs of letting up. The rain has always justified my feelings, made it ok to feel this way. Sometimes when it rains like this it's like the sky is crying and will not stop. The water on my windshield gives the world a whole new look, a makeover of swirling, blended colors with hardly any rhyme or reason to their patterns. The ground appears to be moving, and it sounds as if someone is gently tapping fingers on the roof of my car. The more I write, the harder it rains.

I'm just waiting…waiting for this whole world to flood, to end a generation of disaster. Cultural abortions…. We've had our time. Waiting for it all to wash away.

Medicated Motherfucker

Years have gone by since I've been to the doctor for depression. I went today, to try and get some medication for depression and anxiety. Normally I don't feel 100% anyway, but this work and school schedule has really allowed the stress to flow into my life. With me, stress turns into agitation, agitation turns into anger, and anger eventually manifests itself as depression. I've always liked thinking I could live my entire life like this. However, unless I die at an early age, I can't. The power of all these things is too much. The waves of false emotions overwhelm my senses. Sometimes I don't think I can take it. Writing here is the only thing that gets me by.

I told no one about my upcoming doctor visit, nor will I. Parents, friends—I don't want anyone to know. If they find out, they will only make everything harder, and blow everything out of proportion. I had to laugh. The nurse at the doctor's office asked me, "Are you homicidal? Suicidal?" Of course I said no, because I knew damn well what would happen if I said, "YES! I want to kill everyone!" I bury myself in a world of shit. My entire teen life, I was in a world of shit, and it feels good for once not to be.

My depression is a little different than your whiny-bitch case. I'm not depressed because I think I'm not loved: I have a great family. I know I'm loved. I'm not depressed because of a girl, or a breakup. It seems like this is the number one reason for depression among the younger crowd.

I honestly don't know why I'm depressed, but I think I have a basic idea why. I SOMETIMES feel regret, or remorse, for the ideas and feelings that pass through the halls of my mind. I say sometimes in capital letters because I'm regularly an apathetic guy. Regret, coupled with low serotonin levels, results in depression. I believe it has some genetic basis as well: my dad is the same way. As a matter of fact, my entire family is like this. We are all "Type A" personalities. I need to get put on Xanax or something. I used to take Klonopin, and that worked quite well. However, I was taken off for fear that I would become dependent. Klonopin is highly addictive.

July 23, 2007, is my next appointment. Let's sit back and see what happens.

Insomniac

My chest hurts, my head hurts, my mind is tired, and I'm running on empty. It seems as though I need to get into a relationship every few months just to remind myself why I stopped dating in the first place. This writing is coming out of my insomnia.

Nicole was over last night. She got to my apartment around 1:30 a.m. She was drunk and alone. We sat on the couch together for a while and chit-chatted. I could tell she was in the mood to fool around, so I started kissing her. The smell of her hair, the smoothness of her skin, the softness of her moans. I may not be big on love, but lust is something altogether different. There is nothing more beautiful than the female body. I caressed her for what felt like minutes, when in actuality before I knew it, it was 3:00 a.m. I told her I had to get some sleep. I kissed her goodnight, and she left.

Nicole has left my heart aching, my mind numb, and what emotions I have left crazed. I feel terrible right now. Between thinking about this life, fantasizing about another. and dreaming about Nicole, I'm exhausted. It's as though she has cast a spell on me and I have no control over any and all thoughts and impulses. What's happening to me? The worst part about this whole situation: nothing will come out of these brief encounters, and I will once again be left alone. Angry and pissed off, as I've been so many times before.

Familiar Faces

I had another dream about Dana last night. I've had so many dreams about her, I can't even remember them all. I rarely ever dream about any of my ex-girlfriends. I think that says something. Not only do I miss her, but I loved her. It's sad that years later I still can't forget about her. I was truly happy with her. This shouldn't be bothering me, but every time I have another dream involving Dana, I start thinking about her again. I haven't seen her face in a year, but I still remember what she looks like. Her smile, I remember her bright smile. I loved making her laugh.

After thinking about all of this for a minute, I can't feel anything but anger. I can't feel anything but searing jealousy and anger. It is so fucking pathetic that I can't let any of this go. Do you know why anger is my first reaction? Simply because it's hard to let this go—the feelings of divine FUCKING LOVE, FUCK!

In the end, none of this will change anything. Dana will never read this, nor will I ever see her again. I'll just have to remember this all as a good dream.

I feel so awful right now. Lethargic, irritable and angry…. Fuck.

Nights In White Satin

It sometimes bothers me knowing I'm nothing. Piles of cash and mountains of gold can't and won't alter me. I'm starting to get dizzy… There's no breeze outside—such a muggy day. The music in my ears is swimming around my head, encompassing my entire being, transforming my life into something I'm proud of. Mutating my mind into something I could cherish, leading me to believe I have love in my heart. Making me a "normal person." Normal people don't want to die alone. They may not admit it out loud, but they don't.

I can envision cinematic scenes of love and betrayal being portrayed on my cream-colored walls, filling my room with some type of meaning, some type of value. That is exactly what I do not have. Self esteem is not something I have. Why should I? Who am I? What am I? Unfortunately…nothing. Ha ha, My grandmother tells me I don't give myself enough credit. Credit for what? What have I done to deserve anything?

Misanthrope

"Misanthropy—A hatred or distrust of the human race, or a disposition to dislike and mistrust other people. Misanthropy does not necessarily imply an inhumane, antisocial, or sociopathic attitude towards humanity."

Isn't that something? Haters of the human race may stand before you, and you wouldn't even know it. Holding the door open for you as you enter the bank. Asking you how your weekend was at the gas station counter. Ha ha. The art of deception at its best. It sometimes angers me when people call me a "good person." Sure, I have manners, I'm polite, and when it comes down to it, I'll hold the door open for you. But don't think for one second that I don't hate and despise you to the highest degree beyond reason or logic. I'm by no means a bad person. I do not believe my thoughts are wrong. I do know many people who think I'm a monster. These people, ironically, are even more twisted than myself. Funny how that works.

No End

Until now you've read nothing but pessimistic, negativity, hate-filled notions and angry rants aimed at the world and all of its components. In this date and age, why should that surprise anyone? The world *needs* hate, it needs drama. This world needs despair. Without these things, all that's left is emptiness. What's light without dark? You cannot get rid of your shadow.

When I was a boy, I never saw the hatred I see now. I could not feel it, I could not sense it. That's childhood innocence for you. Nothing wrong with that. Do you remember your childhood? Think back…. Remember those snowball fights with the other neighborhood children? Think about running through life as the summer nights passed you by. It feels like a different life, doesn't it? Like a dream you once had many years ago?

I remember April 19, 1995. That day was a Wednesday. This was the day of the Oklahoma City Bombing. I was seven years old. I remember watching the news footage on television. I remember seeing the plumes of smoke coming from the building. I kept trying to figure out why someone would want to hurt so many people. After many years, I've come to understand why.

Elephant

Emotion on a scale that baffles the mind: Enough serotonin, lithium, and dopamine to last all of ten minutes, and the searing anger of a million empty minds contaminating the world around you. Puts a smile on your face, doesn't it? I've always hated reading the metaphors of others, trying frantically to glue the story together with riddles and rhymes. It still doesn't seem to make any sense.

I'm going to jump around quite a bit if you can't already tell, but in the end, I'll try and link this whole story back to one thing, one concept, one basic point: the complexity, the insanity, the beauty, the horror, and uncertainty of the human mind.

I now live on my own, so on the weekends I am granted the opportunity to wander. Why I just wrote that last sentence, I'm not quite sure. Just looking around right now is making me think… It's hard to comprehend Sundays. It's hard to grasp the setting sun. It's hard to understand the end. It's very easy to be in the dark. It's very easy to be scared. Just remember, your pain is not unique.

Untold Truth

I haven't given much thought to it yet, mainly because it's just happened. The years have snuck up on me, and I didn't even realize it. I'm 20 years old, and I've realized something tonight. My teen years are gone. No longer can this be passed off as "teen angst" or "typical adolescent rage." I have now joined the rest of the sick and diseased, the ones who never grew out of those years. I was always told I would grow out of it. I was lied to.

What made me realize this? My shadow. I was outside smoking a cigarette and I glanced at my shadow. The moon made it look so eerie. When I was a teen, it looked different. I'm still coming to grips with the fact that I'm aging and my prime years are gone. It's hard to watch them pass. For as painful and ridiculous as they were, I miss them. I know in my heart they were the best times I will ever have. Life is now redundant and plain.

Only when I've been drinking would I have noticed something as trivial as this. I suspect most people don't even notice their teen years are gone until they're 40 years old with 4 kids and a mortgage. I've been writing this book for only four years, but it feels like I started it a lifetime ago. I will never be at rest. I'm letting life pass me by.

The End

Where to begin? I suppose I could have started as far back as you wanted me to. But where to end—now that's up to me. I think I've taken you as far I can. From here on out, it's your responsibility, and your duty to figure it all out. I can be of no more assistance.

I hope in your reading you have retained something, and that my writing this book was not done in vain. I don't know what lies ahead for me, and maybe I shouldn't care. I've run out of steam and the train will stop here. Fill me with coal, and hell, who knows? I might actually return again. For some, that maybe enough.

Redundancy is God in my world. This world is a beautiful place. If only there were more beautiful people to fill it. The game of a life is a fucking tragedy, and my opinion of it has yet to change.

I'm not a pessimist, or negative, or any of that other bullshit. I'm a "person" with bullshit problems, just like everyone else. Just like you. Problems…that aren't real. I do try and look at the upside of things I really do, but I can only look so high before my neck begins to crack.